QUICKBOOKS-ONLINE

A Comprehensive Guide to Navigating QuickBooks Online – Understanding, Implementing, and Mastering the Leading Accounting Software

Harrison Grant

Unlock exclusive bonuses by scanning the qr code and share your thoughts with a review!

YOUR FEEDBACK FUELS OUR JOURNEY

Table of Contents

Introduction

Intuit, the brainchild behind the accounting software QuickBooks, has been revolutionizing financial management since 1983. Founded in Mountain View, California, by Scott Cook and Tom Proulx, Intuit initially gained traction with its Quicken program tailored for personal finance. However, recognizing the growing needs of small business owners, Intuit expanded its offerings to include services specifically designed for them.

QuickBooks, Intuit's flagship product, made its debut in 1983, targeting small and medium-sized enterprises. Leveraging the success of Quicken, the initial version of QuickBooks was built upon the Quicken codebase, catering to the burgeoning market of small business proprietors who lacked formal accounting expertise. This early iteration quickly gained popularity, capturing a substantial 85% share of the small business accounting software market in the United States.

Over time, QuickBooks evolved, incorporating cloud-based payroll services, on-premises accounting applications, and payment processing capabilities, catering to the diverse needs of its clientele. Despite its initial success, early versions of QuickBooks faced criticism from professional accountants for lacking robust security measures and compliance with established accounting standards.

To address these concerns and adapt to changing technological landscapes, Intuit introduced QuickBooks Online (QBO), a cloud-based service, in response to the growing demand for flexible and accessible accounting solutions. Unlike its desktop counterpart, QBO operates on a subscription model, offering users the convenience of accessing their financial data securely through a web browser. Intuit ensures regular updates and maintenance of the software, although users may encounter occasional pop-up advertisements for premium services.

QuickBooks Online quickly gained traction in the market, boasting 624,000 subscribers as of May 2014, establishing itself as a frontrunner among online accounting platforms. This success positioned it ahead of competitors like Xero, which had 284,000 clients by July 2014.

Intuit's commitment to innovation was evident in its 2013 declaration of rebuilding QuickBooks Online from the ground up. This overhaul introduced a framework that empowered clients to personalize their online experience and facilitated the development of third-party small business applications, signaling Intuit's dedication to meeting the evolving needs of its users.

Chapter 1:
Introduction to Accounting Software Landscape

What is QuickBooks Online?

QuickBooks Online is a cloud-based accounting platform tailored for small businesses seeking comprehensive financial management solutions. Through its online interface, users gain access to a suite of features including customizable feeds and charts, invoice creation with 'Pay Now' functionality, and mobile compatibility with automatic synchronization. Its native Android and iOS apps empower users with on-the-go capabilities such as sales receipt capture, expense tracking, and real-time cash flow monitoring. Additionally, users can manage accounts, track time, review transactions, and communicate with clients seamlessly.

The platform facilitates collaborative financial analysis by enabling multiple users to access detailed reports and company finances from a unified dashboard. QuickBooks Online streamlines billing and invoicing processes with mobile and print-friendly solutions, alongside tools for trade, profit, and loss sheet generation. Users can tailor their dashboard with personalized reports and feeds, ensuring visibility into the most critical information.

Administrators have the flexibility to add users, adjust permissions, and monitor payments, sales history, and invoice specifics directly from the dashboard. Integration with third-party applications such as Intuit GoPayment, QuickBooks Online Payroll, Shopify, Xero, Salesforce, and Square POS enhances functionality and expands utility for businesses utilizing QuickBooks Online.

Quickbooks Subscription Pricing

There are six distinct versions and price points that come with the online edition of QuickBooks; nevertheless, the majority of users typically select one of these versions regardless of the price point. Check the table below for the pricing;

Version	Monthly	Annually	Users
Self-Employed	$15	$180	1 billable user + 2 accountant users
Simple Start	$30	$360	1 billable user + 2 accountant users
Essentials	$55	$660	3 billable users + 2 accountant users

Plus	$85	$1,020	5 billable users + 2 accountant users
Advanced	$200	$2400	Up to 25 billable users + 3 accountant users
Accountant	$0	$0	No limit

If you choose QuickBooks, you will have the option to select either a free trial for a period of thirty days or a fifty percent discount for the first three months of the subscription that you have selected. In addition, there is a possibility that you may be provided with a discount throughout the trial period of thirty days. If you have any plans to make use of QuickBooks continually, I would advise you to take the plan as you might not have such an offer during the period of your trial. The 50 percent discount will of course save you a lot of money whereas the 30-day trial is an opportunity for you to test the software if it meets all of your needs and more without having to make any form of financial commitment. If you finally decide QuickBooks is not meant for you, you will have to cancel your subscription but the trial will end on the 30th day.

Chapter 2:

Positioning QuickBooks Online in the Market

QuickBooks Online (QBO) stands out in the market as a leading cloud-based accounting software solution, offering a comprehensive suite of features tailored to the needs of small and medium-sized businesses (SMBs) and self-employed professionals. Here's a comparative analysis with its major competitors:

Comparative Analysis with Competitors

Xero

Features: Both QBO and Xero offer robust features for accounting, invoicing, expense tracking, and reporting. However, QBO has a broader range of industry-specific features and integrations, such as inventory management and job costing.

Pricing: QBO's pricing is competitive, especially for its entry-level plans, making it more accessible to startups and small businesses. Xero's pricing starts slightly higher but offers unlimited users in all plans, which can be advantageous for larger teams.

User Experience: Both platforms are known for their user-friendly interfaces, but QBO's integration with other Intuit products like TurboTax and Mint may provide a more seamless user experience for individuals and businesses already using Intuit's ecosystem.

FreshBooks

Features: FreshBooks focuses more on freelancers and service-based businesses, offering features like time tracking and project management alongside basic accounting functionalities. QBO, on the other hand, provides a broader range of features suitable for various industries and business sizes.

Pricing: FreshBooks offers straightforward pricing with fewer tiers, but QBO's scalability and advanced features may justify its slightly higher pricing for businesses with growing needs.

User Experience: Both platforms excel in user experience, with FreshBooks being particularly praised for its simplicity. However, QBO's feature depth and customization options may appeal to businesses requiring more comprehensive accounting solutions.

Wave Accounting

Features: Wave Accounting offers a free accounting solution tailored for very small businesses, but it lacks some of the advanced features and integrations available in QBO. QBO's industry-specific applications and scalability make it a better fit for businesses with more complex needs.

Pricing: While Wave Accounting's free plan is attractive for startups and freelancers, QBO's pricing plans offer more scalability and value for businesses planning for growth.

User Experience: Wave Accounting is known for its simplicity and ease of use, but QBO's user-friendly interface and extensive support resources make it a compelling choice for businesses seeking a more robust accounting solution.

User-Friendly Interface

QuickBooks Online offers a user-friendly interface designed to simplify accounting tasks for users without extensive financial expertise. Here's an examination of its interface along with tips for efficient navigation:

- **Dashboard Overview:** The dashboard provides a snapshot of your business's financial health, displaying key metrics such as income, expenses, and bank account balances.
- **Navigation Bar:** The navigation bar categorizes tasks into logical sections, making it easy to find what you need quickly.
- **Transaction Entry:** QuickBooks Online simplifies transaction entry with customizable templates for recurring transactions.

- **Bank Feeds:** Automatic synchronization of bank transactions simplifies bank reconciliation.
- **Reporting:** Customize reports by adjusting filters and save favorite report settings for future use.
- **Search Functionality:** Use the search bar to quickly locate transactions or other data within QuickBooks Online.
- **Help and Support:** Access tutorials, FAQs, and support articles directly within the platform for assistance with troubleshooting or learning how to use specific features.

Industry-Specific Applications

QuickBooks Online offers industry-specific applications and features tailored to the unique needs of various business sectors. Here are some examples:

- **Retail and E-commerce:** Inventory management, sales tax management, and integration with e-commerce platforms like Shopify.
- **Construction and Contracting:** Job costing, progress invoicing, and contractor management features.
- **Professional Services:** Time tracking, project profitability analysis, and client collaboration tools.
- **Healthcare Practices:** HIPAA compliance, insurance billing, and appointment scheduling integration.
- **Nonprofit Organizations:** Fund accounting, donor management, and grant tracking features.

These industry-specific features make QuickBooks Online a versatile solution that can adapt to the needs of businesses across various sectors, providing tailored solutions to streamline financial processes and improve efficiency.

Chapter 3:

Benefits and Advantages for Businesses

QuickBooks Online (QBO) is a powerful cloud-based accounting software solution that offers numerous benefits and advantages for businesses of all sizes and industries. From simplifying financial management tasks to providing insights for strategic decision-making, QBO empowers businesses to streamline processes, scale efficiently, and drive growth.

Benefits and Advantages for Businesses:

- **Streamlined Financial Management**: QuickBooks Online simplifies accounting tasks such as invoicing, expense tracking, and bank reconciliation, allowing businesses to save time and reduce manual errors.
- **Accessibility and Collaboration**: Being a cloud-based solution, QuickBooks Online enables users to access their financial data anytime, anywhere, and from any device with an internet connection. This facilitates collaboration among team members and advisors, improving communication and efficiency.
- **Cost-Effectiveness**: QuickBooks Online offers subscription-based pricing plans tailored to different business sizes and needs, making it affordable for startups

and small businesses while providing scalability for larger enterprises.

- **Integration Capabilities**: QuickBooks Online integrates with a wide range of third-party apps and business tools, allowing businesses to create a customized ecosystem that meets their unique requirements and enhances productivity.
- **Compliance and Security**: QuickBooks Online helps businesses stay compliant with tax regulations and industry standards while providing robust security measures to protect sensitive financial data.

Case Studies on Process Optimization

E-commerce Business

Challenge: An e-commerce business struggled with manual order processing and inventory management, leading to errors and delays in order fulfillment.

Solution: Implementing QuickBooks Online's integration with e-commerce platforms and inventory management tools streamlined order processing and inventory tracking, reducing errors and improving efficiency.

Results: A considerable reduction in the amount of time required to process orders and an improvement in the precision of inventory were both experienced by the company, leading to higher customer satisfaction and increased sales.

Construction Company

Challenge: A construction company faced challenges with job costing and project profitability analysis, making it difficult to accurately track project expenses and monitor profitability.

Solution: QuickBooks Online's job costing features and customizable reporting capabilities allowed the company to track project expenses in real-time and analyze profitability by project or job.

Results: With improved visibility into project costs and profitability, the construction company was able to make data-driven decisions, optimize resource allocation, and increase overall profitability.

Scalability for Small to Large Enterprises

QuickBooks Online offers scalability that allows businesses to seamlessly grow from small startups to large enterprises. Here's how:

- **Flexible Pricing Plans**: QuickBooks Online offers pricing plans that cater to businesses of all sizes, with the ability to upgrade to higher-tier plans as business needs evolve.
- **Advanced Features**: As businesses grow, QuickBooks Online provides advanced features and capabilities such as multi-entity management, advanced reporting, and user

permissions, ensuring scalability and support for complex business operations.

- **Integration with Enterprise Solutions**: QuickBooks Online integrates with enterprise solutions and platforms, allowing large enterprises to create a cohesive ecosystem that meets their specific requirements and integrates with existing systems.

Advanced Reporting and Analytics

QuickBooks Online offers advanced reporting and analytical capabilities that enable businesses to make informed decisions and drive growth. Here's how businesses can leverage these features:

- **Customizable Reports**: QuickBooks Online allows businesses to create customizable reports tailored to their specific needs, providing insights into key performance indicators, financial trends, and areas for improvement.
- **Visual Dashboards**: Interactive dashboards in QuickBooks Online provide a visual representation of financial data, making it easy for businesses to monitor performance and track progress towards goals.
- **Data Analysis Tools**: QuickBooks Online offers data analysis tools such as trend analysis, variance analysis, and forecasting, empowering businesses to identify patterns, predict future outcomes, and make proactive decisions.

By leveraging the advanced reporting and analytical capabilities of QuickBooks Online, businesses can gain a deeper understanding of their finances, identify opportunities for growth, and drive strategic decision-making.

Chapter 4:

Creating a QuickBooks Online Company

When you log in to QuickBooks Online, you'll be prompted to create your company profile. You can start by entering your data from scratch, or if applicable, import it from QuickBooks Desktop. Additionally, you can import lists such as customers, vendors, and inventory items.

Signing Up for QuickBooks Online

Once you've decided to use QuickBooks for your company, it's important that your online activities accurately reflect your real-world transactions. This includes tracking sales, managing bank deposits, and handling other financial tasks. While some actions, like invoicing, are done entirely within QuickBooks, most of the transactions you record occur elsewhere.

Ensure that your accounting captures each step of every transaction, whether it involves credit card payments, payroll processing through QuickBooks Payroll, or securing a bank loan. This means reconciling recorded transactions with your actual bank statements, verifying names, dates, payment methods, and amounts.

Here's how to sign up for QuickBooks Online:

1. Visit quickbooks.intuit.com/pricing.

2. Look for the four subscription options: Simple Start, Essentials, Plus, and Advanced. If you're a freelancer or independent contractor interested in QuickBooks Self-Employed, scroll down past the main options.

3. Choose between a 30-day free trial or discounted prices for three months on Simple Start, Essentials, and Plus. Note that Advanced doesn't offer a free trial, but you can access a demo at qbo.intuit.com/redir/testdrive_us_advanced.

4. If opting for a free trial, toggle the slider button for your chosen QuickBooks version. Keep in mind that purchasing the software immediately saves more and incurs lower subscription fees, as discounts don't apply to free trials. Also, promotional pricing typically ends after three months.

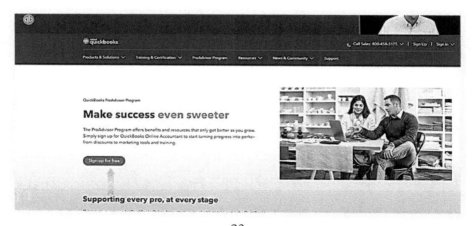

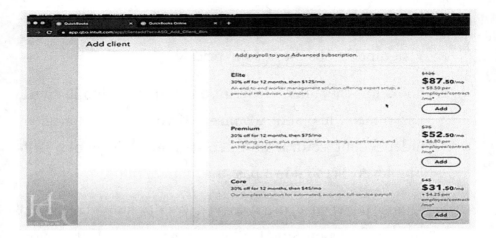

Exploring Your New Company

In QuickBooks Online, companies exhibit similar traits to those found in conventional businesses. Here are a few of these attributes:

1. Access your company's dashboard by logging into your QuickBooks account.

2. Navigate to Account and Settings by clicking the gear icon.

3. Then, select the Company tab within the Account and Settings section.

Company Name Modification

1. To change the company name, simply click within the designated area where the company name is displayed, including the pencil icon.

2. After making the necessary adjustments, click on the Save button.

Adding Company Logo

Within the company name section, there is an option to include your company logo. For the purpose of importing it into QuickBooks Online, follow the instructions below:

1. Click on the gray square next to the company logo.

2. If your logo has been previously uploaded to QuickBooks Online, it will be displayed on the screen. Choose to include it in your company's details. If the desired logo isn't shown, click the blue plus sign to add it.

3. QuickBooks will prompt you to browse your computer and select the logo image file.

   o Click Open to return to the previous screen and preview a thumbnail of your new logo after selecting the image file.

4. Once the desired logo is highlighted, click on the Save button to store it in your QuickBooks Online account. This ensures that you won't need to refresh it when customizing forms.

Company and Legal Name

Please specify your company name exactly as you want it to appear on forms and invoices. Ensure that the name provided matches the official business name registered with the IRS. For tax-related documents like Form 1099 and payroll tax returns, the legal name will be utilized. If your legal name differs from the company name you wish to display on invoices, please uncheck the box and enter your legal name.

EIN: Your IRS-provided number should align with this. If you're self-employed, use your Social Security number. As EINs are sensitive information, QuickBooks may prompt you to verify your login before accessing or editing the EIN.

Type of Company

To input or modify your company type details:

1. Click the pencil icon or any other location within the Company Type section.

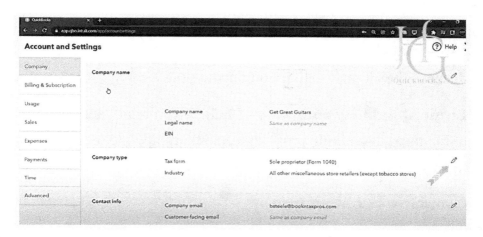

2. Select your taxable entity type from the drop-down menu next to the Tax form field by clicking on it.

Sole Proprietorship: If you are the only person running your business, you are a lone proprietor. Use Schedule C to report any income or losses (Form 1040).

Partnership: If you run your firm with two or more partners, choose this business category. Form 1065 is used by partnerships to report their business's profits and losses.

S corporation (S-corp): A corporation that chooses to be an S-corp reports on Form the 1120S and transfers corporate income, loss, and taxes through to its shareholders.

A c corporation (C-corp): Rather than going through to the owners, a corporation that meets the requirements to be a C-corp is taxed independently from them. C-corps file reports using Form 1120.

Nonprofit organization: Nonprofits are tax-exempt businesses that prioritize social goals over financial gain. They disclose their yearly activity on Form 990.

Limited liability company (LLC): If you're not sure whether to file taxes as a single proprietor, partnership, or S-corp, choose this company structure.

Company's Contact Info

- To enter **contact details for QuickBooks and your clients**, click **anywhere** in the Contact info section, including the pencil symbol.

Email: The email address that QuickBooks will use to get in touch with the administrator is your business email. Your clients' sales forms, like invoices, will include the customer-facing email address. Uncheck the option and enter the proper address if this is different from the QuickBooks administrator's email address.

Company Phone: Enter the phone number that will be printed on the sales forms consumers receive.

Website: For it to appear on all of your sales forms, enter a website address.

Company Address

To input or modify your company's address information, click the pencil icon or any other location in the address area. The corporate address, customer-facing address, and legal address are all listed separately in this QuickBooks Online version.

Company address: The firm address, which serves as the business's physical address, is what you use to send payments to QuickBooks.

- Click **Save** after making the necessary adjustments.

Customer-facing address: This address, which can be seen on your invoices and other sales documents, should be where clients should send their payments. Uncheck the box and input the right customer-facing address if it differs from your corporate address. For modifications to be saved,

- click **Save**.

Legal address: Your tax filings must be sent to the legal address, which must coincide with the address you have on record with the IRS. Again, you must uncheck the option and provide the legal address if this is different from the company address.

- Once you're satisfied with the address you've entered, simply click the Save button highlighted in green.

Reviewing the Quickbooks Interface

If you're a seasoned Desktop user, the differences between QuickBooks Desktop and Online can be rather noticeable. But we can't just base everything on appearances!

Some desktop users switching to QuickBooks Online could encounter a challenging learning curve. Although they have identical functionality, the two different systems that they are intended to run on have different interfaces. Once mastered, however, QuickBooks Online's more streamlined design may make your accounting simpler than QuickBooks Desktop. It only requires a grasp of the layout.

Your emphasis will be split between the header bar and the navigation bar as you navigate QuickBooks Online.

Header Bar

The header bar, which runs along the top and has navigation options to the right, appears once you have logged into the QuickBooks Online service.

We have access to anything we need to enter by using the "+ icon." Consider this the location to use when introducing any new types of transactions. Our Customers, Vendors, Employees, and Others are clearly categorized in the frame that appears. It helps to consider these as transactions of the incoming payment variety, goods that need to be paid off, payroll, and adjusting/banking entries. This resembles the flowchart on QuickBooks Desktop's home page!

The "gear icon" provides entry to various features for your company file, including budgeting, audit logging, settings adjustment, limits configuration, and import/export capabilities.

Navigation Bar

The user interface's left side is occupied by a vertical navigation bar that provides rapid access to QuickBooks' features.

- **Banking**: gives access to locations that can immediately download information and display matches for past bank transactions and bill payments. This function is more useful than the desktop version because it doesn't open a new window but instead displays Name, Account, Customer, and Class in a drop-down menu. There is still a "Batch Actions" option to add new transactions to the bank register if the system has correctly identified transactions. The best feature of QuickBooks Online bank feeds is the ability to check previously inserted or matched transactions and undo them if an error was made.

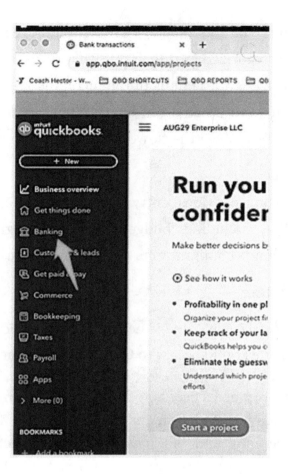

- **Sales**: access to the Customer Center, which contains information on your clients, invoices, products, and services. Live charts that are updated in real-time at the top of these sections display which clients/invoices are past due and which goods are running low on stock. Although it doesn't replace reporting, this toolbar is an excellent method to quickly monitor your business.

- **Expenses**: gives access to information about vendors and expenses. A running tally of open and past-due bills still appears at the top along with vendor information. To make it apparent which account the invoices and expenses are going to, the account is displayed as a category under the expenses tab. This is a fantastic tool to make sure expenses are entered properly for each individual vendor.

- **Workers**: gives contractors and employees access to payroll. The system performs an excellent job of displaying which suppliers are contractors (a check box situated in the vendor description section) and the amount paid out, as was already mentioned. If your business employs a lot of contractors, QuickBooks Online enables regular check-ins to ensure that all pertinent information has been gathered, which makes filing time a snap.
- **Reports**: gives you access to all reporting features and any customized reports you may have saved in your favorites. All your overview, A/P, A/R, employee, and other reports will be gathered together to assist you to identify the report that is most suited for your purposes in the online edition, which strives to organize everything by what you need.

The fact that checks and deposits cannot be input directly into a bank register in QuickBooks Online is a major distinction. The Online edition of QuickBooks demands that transactions be entered individually via the "+ icon" in the header bar, despite the fact that this would appear as a convenient option in QuickBooks Desktop.

It is true that this method requires more time. When using QuickBooks Desktop, it can be simple to scroll through new entries in the register and unintentionally make mistakes that end up costing your company money. The QuickBooks Online approach of inputting transactions one at a time slows down bookkeepers enough to evaluate the work and possibly spot errors before they snowball rather than having them rush through a register. This extra time spent upfront can prevent spending even more time later on locating and correcting errors.

Chapter 5:
Customer, Vendor and Employee Lists

Lists are used by QuickBooks Online, just as the QuickBooks Desktop product, to help you save background data that you'll utilize repeatedly. For the most part, you will be entering information regarding the individuals with whom you conduct business, including customers, vendors, and staff, as well as the products that you purchase or sell. However, you also save lists of other data that is in the background, including the accounts your business utilizes and the payment methods it takes.

Adding New Records to a List

The links Sales, Expenses, and Workers in the Navigation bar are used to interact with your clients, suppliers, staff members, and subcontractors. When starting the process of including a new customer, you need only select the appropriate link from the navigation bar. This link can be found under Sales for customers, Expenses for vendors, and Workers for employees and contractors, vendor, employee, or contractor. Continue reading to discover how to set up a new client.

Creating A New Record

In this section that has to do with creating a new record, I will be making use of customers as an example since you definitely cannot do without establishing a customer as they are the soul of a business. Additionally, you can create sub-customers and designate customer types for customers; however, vendors, employees, and other third parties cannot use these functions.

Follow the steps below to set up a new customer in QuickBooks Online;

If you have established that your company needs to use the Multicurrency option, you should make sure that it is activated before you begin producing individuals. The availability of the fields that are necessary to establish the currency of each individual will be ensured as a result of this.

1. Select **Sales** in the **Navigation bar** then choose **Customers** in order to show the Customers page.

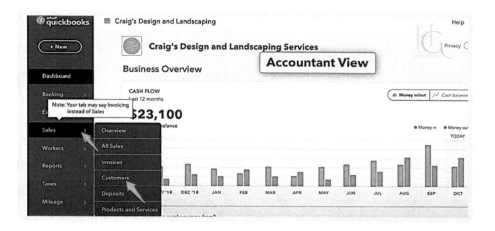

2. Select the **New Customer** button located in the upper right corner of the page.

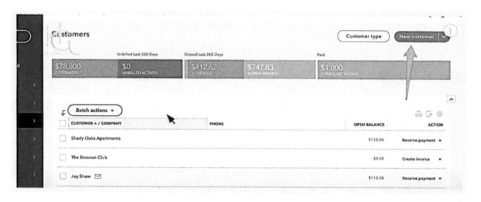

3. Insert the **necessary information** as requested.

4. Finally click on the **Save button.**

Due to the fact that you only just added the customer, you will not be able to view any transactions until QBO saves the customer and displays the customer's page with transaction information that is pertinent to that customer. You will also have the ability to examine and amend the information that you have just created for the customer if you choose the option that indicates Customer Details. It is possible to re-display the whole list of clients by first clicking Sales in the navigation bar and then clicking Sales again.

As long as the related person has a balance of $0, you are able to make any client, supplier, or contractor inactive. Click the Action down arrow next to the entry on the right side of the relevant list to render someone inactive. Click Make Inactive in the list that appears.

Using Customer Types

You can organize otherwise unrelated clients into customer kinds; for instance, maybe you provide some customers exclusive discounts at particular periods of the year. You can use a customer type to make it easier for you to decide which customers will receive the discount.

1. Click the **Customer Types button** in the top right corner of the **Customers page** to create new customer types.

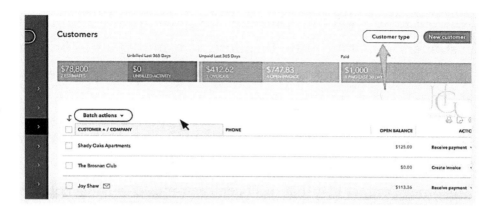

2. Next, give your customer type a name and click **Save**. Repeat these steps for each new customer type you want to create.

3. Click the **customer's name** on the **Customers page**, then select the b tab to designate a customer category.

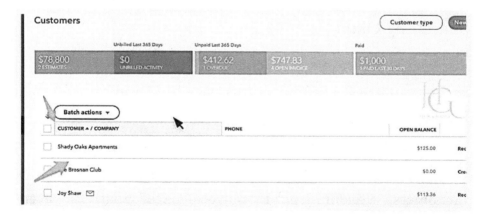

4. To re-display the dialog box, click the **Edit button** at the top or on the right side of the **Customer Details page**. In that dialog box, select the **Additional Info tab** to give the customer a customer category.

It is possible to allocate the same customer type to a group of customers simultaneously; therefore, it is important to bear in mind that you do not have to give the customer type to every customer individually in order to save time.

Utilize the Sales by Customer Type Detail report, the Sales by Customer Detail report that is grouped by customer type, and the Customer Contact List that has been customized to add a column for the customer type in order to view your customers in accordance with their designated customer type.

Working with Records

This section will highlight some of the many records that may be used with QuickBooks online as well as how to use them.

Searching Lists

The pages for customers, vendors, and employees can all be used in different ways. The Contractors page has fewer features than the others; you can use it to look for contractors and create 1099s. You can sort the list of individuals, export the list to Excel, and take actions on a certain subset of individuals on the list from the Customers, Vendors, or Employees pages that list every individual in those categories.

On any listing page, you can print a simple report by

- selecting the **Print button**, which is located directly above the **Action column**.

Accessing Attachments

To maintain track of crucial financial data, you can attach files. You can include things like a customer's contract, a vendor's 1099 form, or an employee's receipt. You have the option to submit images in addition to text documents.

1. Simply **drag and drop the item** into the **Attachments box** located at the bottom left of the relevant details page.

2. Alternatively, you can **click the box** to bring up the typical **Windows Open dialog box,** allowing you to navigate to and choose the attachment you want to use.

   Each attachment is limited to 25MB in size.

3. Click the **Show Existing** link below the **Attachments box** to examine papers you've already attached to a person. QBO will then open a pane on the right side of the page with the associated attachments.

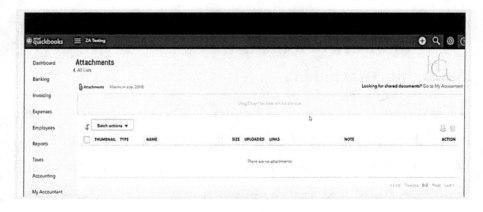

Adding attachments to a transaction is another option. You must add the Attachments column to the table on the person's Transaction List page in order to view transactions that have attachments.

1. Click the table gear button above the Action column to display the person's Transaction List page.

2. Pick Show More from the list that appears. When you click the Attachments check box, the Show More setting changes to Show Less, and the Attachments column is added to the table grid.

With a paperclip, you can identify it as the column heading. When the Attachments column is displayed for one person, it is also displayed for all individuals of that kind in the Transaction List database. You can view the number of attachments for any given transaction in the column if there are any. The attachments for the transaction are listed when you click the number; clicking one of the attachments in the list opens it.

You add attachments to the various transactions as you create them; only attachments related to transactions and attachments associated with a person appear on the relevant person's page and the various Transaction List pages.

Sorting A List on The Customers and Vendors Page

The lists on the Customers and Vendors page can be sorted by name or open balance in addition to the Split View sorting options. By default, QBO arranges the entries on these pages in ascending alphabetical order by name.

Employees can be sorted by status, pay type, alphabetical order, and reverse alphabetical order (active or inactive). Contractors cannot be sorted; by default, QBO arranges them alphabetically.

1. To access the appropriate page, select **Sales or Expenses** from the **Navigation bar,** then click on **Customers or Vendors**. For the sake of this demonstration, I will select the Customers page on the website. By doing so, you will

be able to alter the order in which the **lists of Customers or Vendors** are arranged.

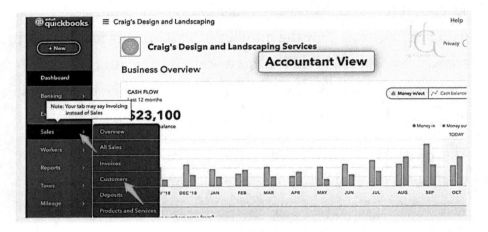

2. After that, click **the heading of the column** you want to order by. When you click the heading for the **Customer/Company** column in **QBO**, the customers are listed in descending alphabetical order starting from the top.

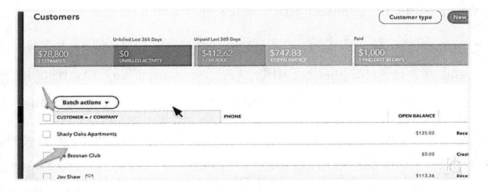

3. **QBO** arranges the list in **Open Balance order,** from lowest to highest, if you click the column heading for that column.

Working with A Batch of Records

When working with clients or suppliers, you can execute certain actions simultaneously for a collection of records.

Changing Setting for Lists

The lists on the Customers page, Vendors page, and Employees page can all be modified to some extent. You may decide whether to display or hide the information like street addresses, attachments, emails, and phone numbers, not to mention the question of whether or not to bring in inactive entries on the list for inclusion. Additionally, you can decide how many entries are shown on each page and how wide the columns are for those entries.

Based on the list in use, certain sections can be revealed or concealed. For example, you have the option to display or withhold address details for customers and vendors, while maintaining transparency for employees or contractors.

To view the linked page,

1. select the relevant link from the Navigation bar (Sales, Expenses, or Employees).

2. To make changes to the information that is displayed in the list, click the table Gear button that is located above the Action column on the right side of the page. To show or hide information, check boxes can then be selected or deselected.

3. When done, click outside the list.

I advise you to **click in the open space** at the bottom of the Navigation bar when you click outside the list to avoid unintentionally leaving the current page.

Accessing Other Lists

By selecting the gear symbol for Settings in the Heading, you may access lists. Lists is one of the categories that appear.

- Click All Lists under the Lists category.

After that, a page of lists will appear. There are lists for Recurring Transactions, Product Categories, Custom Form Styles, Payment Methods, Terms, and Attachments in addition to the Chart of Accounts Products, and Services.

You can quickly return to the list view by

- selecting **All Lists** from the breadcrumb navigation under the title after choosing any list to open it in full table format. This course will begin with a look at the list of recurring transactions.

Chapter 6:

Invoicing Customers and Receiving Payments

The excitement begins right here because the topics covered in this chapter have to do with raising capital, which is the most enjoyable aspect of running a business from the standpoint of any businessperson.

Getting Oriented with Sales Transactions

You can see the status of sales transactions, open invoices, and paid invoices very clearly on the Sales page. From within the page, you can also examine, make, and edit sales transactions.

- Go to Bookkeeping, Transactions, and then All Sales, or go to Sales and then All Sales, to go to this page.

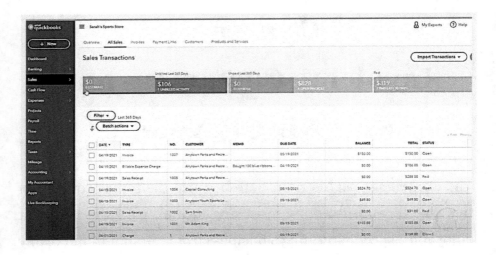

View Transaction and Invoice Status at A Glance

The Money Bar, a crucial element of the Sales page, will be visible after you go there. It provides you with a fast view of open and recently paid invoices and quickly displays the status and dollar amounts of your sales transactions. Additionally, it displays any unbilled fees, charges, time activities, or estimates.

The list allows you to view information about certain transactions and can show:

- Estimates
- Invoices
- Sales receipts
- Payments
- Credit memos
- Delayed charges (for QuickBooks Online Plus, Advanced, and Essentials only)

- Billable time activities (QuickBooks Online Plus and Advanced only)

The list makes it simple to see any transaction's status and determine if it is Open, Closed, Paid, Partially Paid, or Overdue.

The list is easily customizable so that you can view the data you require:

- To see only the items you are interested in, filter the list.
- View only the info you require by altering the columns.
- In order to work with the data included in lists in different ways, export lists to Microsoft Excel.

Keep in mind that '365 days' is the default view for all transactions. If an invoice was not created during the previous 365 days, the Invoices page won't show up.

Managing sales transactions from the sales page is very easy as you will be able to;

1. From the New transaction dropdown menu, create new invoices, payments, sales receipts, estimates, credit memos, delayed charges, and billable time activity.

2. Do anything about a transaction. For instance, by choosing Receive Payment in the Action column, you can pay an invoice right away from the list.

3. Print transactions or packing slips, either for a specific group or an individual (for invoicing and sales receipts).

4. Delete, invalidate, or copy transactions.

5. Send transactions, and when sending just one, personalize the message that goes with it.

6. Update the estimations' status.

7. Expand consumer entries to include additional details like charges, time spent on activities, and credits (exclusive to QuickBooks Online Plus, Advanced, and Essentials versions).

Creating Invoices

Send your customers an invoice if you expect to get paid for the goods and services you provide in the future. You can include the good or service you're selling in an invoice that you send to your client via email.

I'll demonstrate how to make new invoices as well as how to look through outstanding debts. We'll also provide information on how to manage things if you utilize an external payment processing platform like QuickBooks Payments, where clients can pay their invoices online.

Step 1: Create and Send an Invoice

Using the Old Experience

1. Click on **New**.

2. Choose **Invoice**.

3. Choose **a customer** from the **Customer dropdown menu**. Verify that every piece of information, including the email address, is accurate.

4. Check the **invoice's date**. Modify the due date within the Terms dropdown if needed. The term "net" indicates the number of days until payment is required. Adjustments to the due date are permissible; the default setting is 30 days.

5. Choose **a product or service** from the **Product/Service column**.

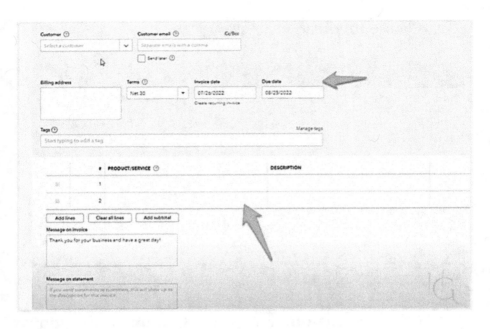

6. If necessary, enter a quantity, rate, and amount change.

7. If you must charge sales tax, tick the Tax box.

8. When finished, you have a number of options for saving or distributing the invoice:

   o When you're prepared to email your customer with the invoice, choose Save and send. If necessary, edit the email, then click **Send and close**.
   o Select **Save and close** to send the invoice at a later time.
   o Choose **Save** to print a printed invoice. Choose Print or Preview next.
   o Choose **Save and share a link** if you want to SMS your customer a link to their invoice.

Step 2: Review Unpaid Invoices

Unpaid invoices are added to your accounts receivable account by QuickBooks. This account will appear on your balance sheet as well as other financial reports.

- Go to **Get paid & pay or Sales & costs**, then **pick Invoices** whenever you wish to check your invoices. To find out where invoices stand in the sales process, look at the Status column.

Here are a few typical states you might encounter:

- **Due in (days)**: the email has not been invoiced yet.
- **Due in (days) Sent**: the invoice has been sent to the customer.
- **Due in (days) Viewed**: the customer has opened the invoice.
- **Deposited**: invoice has been paid by the customer.
- **Overdue (days)**: the invoice is past the due date and has not been paid.
- **Overdue (days) Viewed**: the customer opened the invoice but hasn't paid the past-due invoice.
- **Delivery issue**: The invoice was not delivered. You might have to check the email address and attempt sending it again.
- **Voided**: The invoice was voided in QuickBooks.

Step 3: Receive Payments for Invoices

Clients have the option to settle their invoices effortlessly through either credit card or ACH transfer with QuickBooks Payments. All processing and administrative tasks are handled seamlessly for you. QuickBooks automatically logs transactions into the relevant accounts upon payment reception.

You can monitor payments made through an external platform in QuickBooks if you do so.

Creating Billable Time Entries

You must enable the billable time setting if you wish to charge your client straight from the monitored time. This is how:

1. Choose Settings. Select Account and settings after that.

2. Choosing the Time tab.

3. Select Edit from the Timesheet section.

4. Activate the setting that says "Allow time to be billed."

5. Select **Show billing** rate to users entering the time checkbox if you want your users to see their billable rate when they enter their time. If you bill clients at a different hourly rate than you pay your employees and subcontractors, you might wish to leave this unchecked.

6. Choose **Save**, then choose **Done**.

You can then create a billable time through the Time tab:

1. Select **Time**, then **Time entries**, under **Payroll**.

2. Choose the user for whom you are adding time, then click **Add Time**.

3. If necessary, change the date range in the menu by selecting **This week, Last week, or Custom**. Next, choose the day for which you are entering time.

4. To enter a start time and end time, turn on the Start/end times switch and add the number of hours worked.

5. Choosing **Add work details**. Next, choose your customer or project from the **Customer/Project dropdown**.

6. Switch on **Billable (/hr)** to make the timesheet billable.

7. Add any necessary choices or notes.

8. Choose **Done**.

9. Select **Add** and repeat steps 4 through 8 if you need to add more timesheets for that employee.

10. Click on the **Save and Close option**.

Entering Time Activities

You can record the total number of hours worked by your employee or vendor for the week on weekly timesheets.

Note:

- Timesheets for each week are not posted transactions. This means that until the contents of the timesheets have been included in a sale for an expense-type transaction, they will not appear on reports like Profit and Loss.
- There can be only one hourly rate per timesheet. You can subscribe to QBO Payroll if you need to enter several hourly rates.

Follow the steps below to complete this process;

1. Choose + New.

2. Select Weekly Timesheet under Employees.

CUSTOMERS	VENDORS	EMPLOYEES	OTHER
Invoice	Expense	Payroll	Bank deposit
Receive payment	Check	Single time activity	Transfer
Estimate	Bill	Weekly timesheet	Journal entry
Credit memo	Pay bills	Approve time	Statement
Sales receipt	Purchase order		Inventory qty adjustme
Refund receipt	Vendor credit		Pay down credit card
Delayed credit	Credit card credit		Apply for Capital

3. Choose **the employee or vendor's name** and the week you want to record from the little arrow icons.

4. Fill in the remaining fields. Note: Click **Settings** under the **Total Hours** to adjust the days available.

   o **Customer or project**: choose the customers or project you would like to bill the activity to or you can also choose to track expenses.

   o **Service**: Choose the service that represents the activity.

   o **Billable**: Choose the checkbox and insert the rate if there is a need for you to bill the activity to the customer.

   o **Location and class**: ensure this feature is turned on.

   o **Description**: Insert a description activity.

   o **Time field**: Insert the number of hours and minutes your employee or vendor spent working on this activity.

5. Finally, click on **Save**.

Adding Billable Time and Expenses to An Invoice

You can send consumers invoices for particular project-related costs after creating projects (including timesheets). These procedures apply whether you bill consumers a fixed price or a time and materials fee.

Step 1: Decide How You Will Like to Be Charged for Projects

If you bill for time and materials, you typically invoice clients for the precise costs and labor hours associated with a certain project. To include them in invoices, you must make your project expenses and timesheets billable.

Usually, you don't invoice for specific project expenses if you charge a fixed rate. Instead, you provide consumers with a project-wide estimate. When the work starts, you can turn the estimate into an invoice.

You might occasionally need to charge for particular project expenses, though. One typical instance is when clients request additional work that wasn't originally part of the project plan.

Step 2: Switch on Billable Expenses

If you have not already, turn on billable expenses.

1. Click Account and settings under Settings.

2. Choosing the Expenses tab.

3. To expand it, go to the Bills & Expenses area and pick it.

4. The Make expenses and items chargeable switch should be turned on.

5. To save and then exit your settings, select Save and then Done.

Step 3: Make Project Expenses Billable

- Navigate to Business overview then click on **Projects** and then open the specific project.

Project Expenses

1. Select Choose Add to Project, then Expense.

2. Fill out the form with expenditures.

3. Each item's Billable box should be checked.

4. Select Publish and close.

5. From the Customer/Project dropdown menu, choose the project.

6. Choose Save.

Project Timesheets

1. Choose + **New**.

2. Click on the **Time entry**.

3. Select a **worker**.

4. Choose **a day and, if necessary, adjust the date range**.

5. To input a start time and end time for that day, turn Start/end times on. Alternatively, enter the number of hours worked.

6. Select **To add the project** and make the timesheet billable, provide work information.

   o If there is a need for you to make use of a custom rate for this timesheet, click on **Use custom** rate then insert your preferred amount.

7. Click on **Done**.

8. Click on Save and Close.

Keep in mind that your staff members can directly link their time to the project you created if you utilize QuickBooks Time. In order for those timesheets to display in your project, make sure you approve and export them.

Step 4: Invoice Your Customer for Billable Expenses

Return to the project's Overview tab after making all of your project expenses and timesheets chargeable.

1. Select **Invoice** after choosing **Add to Project**.

2. From the **Customer dropdown menu**, choose the **client you want to invoice**.

3. Your timesheets and chargeable expenses will show up in the **Add to the Invoice section**. All time and chargeable expenses should be added to the invoice.

4. Finish up with the invoice, then **submit it to your client**.

If you wish to submit timesheets or specific expenses as an invoice:

1. Enter your **project now.**

2. Head over to the **Transactions tab**.

3. Locate the timesheet or chargeable expense on the list.

4. Select **From the Action column**, choose to **Create Invoice**.

5. Finish the invoice, then submit it to your client.

Printing a Batch of Invoices or Packing Slips

When shipping items to customers, a packing slip is a document that lists the item, quantity, and other crucial shipping details.

Print A Packing Slip in Quickbooks Online

1. Select Customers under Customers & leads.

2. To get a list of the customer's transactions, click on their name.

3. Choose the checkbox next to each invoice or sales receipt for which you wish to print a packing slip from the Transaction List tab.

4. Print packing slip after selecting the Batch operations selection.

5. You can choose printing choices, examine a preview, and print from the print preview screen.

Recording Customer Payments

You enter a customer's payment into QBO after receiving it. The following options are available for displaying the Receive Payment window:

1. Find the invoice for which you wish to record a payment in the **Sales Transactions list**, and then click **Receive Payment in the Action column**.

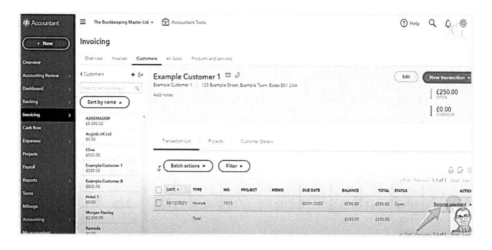

2. On the Sales Transactions page, you can click the New Transaction button and choose Payment.

3. You can choose Receive Payment by clicking the Create menu.

4. Choose Projects, choose the project you're working on, and then click Add to Project.

When you select the first option from the preceding list, QBO opens the Receive Payment window with the details of the selected invoice and a suggested payment amount already filled in.

When using the second or third approach, QBO shows a blank Receive Payment window. After selecting a customer, the Outstanding Transactions section will appear at the bottom of the window, displaying all open bills associated with that customer.

- Choose a **payment method** at the top of the screen, then choose the account you want QBO to deposit the customer's payment into. The sum of the client's payment should be entered in the **Amount Received column**. Check the box next to each invoice that has been paid with the customer's payment in the section titled **Outstanding Transactions**.

Understanding the Payments to Deposit account

Credit card and ACH payments processed using QuickBooks Payments are deposited into the chosen external bank account. You can think of this as your payments account.

The external bank account that QuickBooks uses to deposit payments can easily be changed. Keep in mind that you can only use one account to collect payments at once.

Change Your Payments Account

To use QuickBook Payments, follow the instructions for the QuickBooks product you are using. Two primary account settings are as follows:

Standard deposit: By entering your bank routing and account number, you can connect a bank account for customary funding occasions (non-instant deposits).

Updating the Standard Deposit account

1. Open QuickBooks Online using a web browser; do not use GoPayments or the mobile app.

2. Go to Settings menu and select "Account and settings."

3. Choose the Payments tab, then click on "Change bank" under Standard Deposits in the Deposits section.

4. Select "Create a new bank account."

5. To modify your bank account, enter the routing number and account number.

6. Once you've entered the details, click "Save."

7. Before finalizing your request, review the bank account information to ensure accuracy.

Instant Deposit: connect a debit card to finance Instant Deposit transactions. The debit card associated with your QuickBooks Cash account is already set up.

Updating the Instant Deposit account

1. Navigate to Settings, then select Account and Settings.

2. Scroll down to the Payments tab and find the Deposit accounts section.

3. Click on Change to update your instant deposit details.

4. Opt for the 0% fee option if switching from your personal debit card to your QuickBooks Cash debit card.

5. Once done, click Save and then Done to confirm the changes.

Customer payments from online invoicing and other sources will begin to be deposited into the new account by QuickBooks.

Remember that this does not alter how payments are categorized by QuickBooks on your chart of accounts. This modifies the bank account that QuickBooks uses to deposit funds.

Recording Invoice Payments

You can make and send an invoice to your client if they intend to pay you in the future. In order to balance your accounts, you must record customer payments and link them to the appropriate invoices.

Please take note: If you process payments with QuickBooks Payments, we take care of the accounting for you. QuickBooks processes the money and assigns it to the appropriate account when your customer pays the invoice.

To mark an invoice as paid, you must record the customer payment after processing it in QuickBooks. If not, the invoice is left open and shows up on your records as underpaid. An invoice can be paid in full or in part, and QuickBooks keeps track of any unpaid amount.

Single Invoice

1. Click on the "+ New" button.

2. Select "Receive Payment."

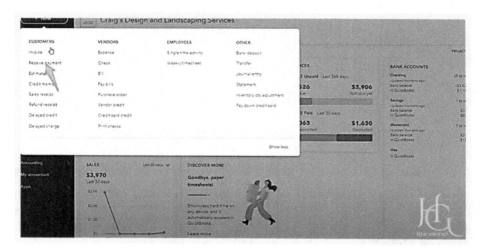

3. Pick the customer's name from the Customer dropdown menu.

4. Choose payment method from the Payment method dropdown.

5. Select account you wish to deposit the money into from the Deposit to dropdown menu.

6. Check the box next to the invoice you are recording the payment for in the Outstanding Transactions section.

7. Enter Memo and Reference number if needed.

8. Finally, click on "Publish and Close."

Recording Partial Payment for An Invoice

1. Choose + **New.**

2. Choosing to **Receive payment**.

3. Choose **customer's name** from the **Customer dropdown menu**.

4. Choose payment method from the **Payment method dropdown**.

5. Choose account you want to deposit the money into from the **Deposit to drop-down menu.**

6. Put your customer's payment amount in the **Amount received column**.

7. Choose the checkbox next to the invoice for which you are recording the payment in the **Outstanding Transactions section**.

8. If necessary, enter the **Memo and Reference number**.

9. Select **Publish and close**.

QuickBooks applies the payment to the invoice line items in order when you record partial payments. Up until the payment is finished, additional payments are applied to the subsequent line items.

Having More Than One Payment in A Single Deposit

Use the Undeposited Funds account to record the payments in QuickBooks if you deposit multiple checks into the bank at once. This enables you to combine numerous payments into a single

QuickBooks deposit transaction. Do this only if your bank combines several payments into one deposit.

Entering A Sales Receipt

If you opt for a different Point of Sale system, you have the option to input a consolidated daily sales receipt in QuickBooks. Alternatively, if you overlook sending invoices to clients, this method can help you save time without compromising the accuracy of your income reports. Here's a detailed guide to help you begin:

Step 1: Establish A Customer Profile for Daily Sales.

This customer account is exclusively designated for your "end of day" sales receipt.

1. Choose Customers from Get paid & pay or Sales by going there.

2. Choose New customer.

3. Specify Daily Sales.

4. Choose Save.

Step 2: Set Up Accounts for Daily Sales

Ensure that the accounting for your daily sales are upright. You can declare your income accurately by doing this to a great extent.

Setting up daily sales accounts entails:

1. On the Toolbar, choose the **Gear icon**.

2. Select **Chart of Accounts** from the **Your Company menu**.

3. Click **New** in the top right corner.

4. Get these accounts set up:

Name	Category Type/ Account Type	Detail Type	Description
Daily Sales Income	Income	Other Primary Income/Sales of Product Income	For tracking daily sales
Clearing account	Cash and cash equivalents	Bank / Cash on hand	Zero balance account for daily sales
Overage and Underage expense	Expense	Other Business Expenses	For drawer shortages

Step 3: Set Up Items for Daily Sales

To keep your things organized, create a category called "Daily Sales":

1. On the **Toolbar**, choose the **Gear icon**.

2. Select **All Lists** from the **Lists menu.**

3. Choose the preferred **Product categories** you want.

4. In the top right corner, choose **New Category.**

5. The new category is called **Daily Sales**.

6. Choose **Save**.

After the Category has been set up, the following items will be implemented:

1. On the Toolbar, choose the **Gear icon**.

2. Select **Products and Services** from the **Lists section**.

3. Click **New** in the top right corner.

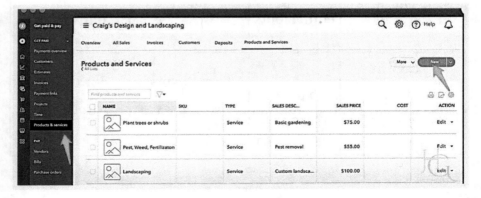

4. Set these things up. Note: For each item, be sure to choose **Daily Sales as the Category**.

Step 4: Create A Daily Sales Template

To maintain a record of daily total sales, follow these steps using the provided template:

1. Navigate to the Toolbar and click on the Gear icon.

2. Choose "Recurring Transactions" from the options displayed.

3. Click on "New" located in the top right corner.

4. From the dropdown menu for Transaction Type, select "Sales Receipt."

5. Ensure the Type is set to "Unscheduled" and designate the template name as "Daily Sales."

6. Assign "Daily Sales" as the client.

7. The following items should be chosen in the Product/Service section;

   o Daily Sales: Daily Sales Income
   o Daily Sales: Cash
   o Daily Sales: Check
   o Daily Sales: Visa/Mastercard
   o Daily Sales: American Express
   o Daily Sales: Overage/Underage

      o   Daily Sales: Discover

8. Click on **Save template**.

Step 5: Record Your Total Daily Sales

Your sales receipt template is now ready. Your "end of day" sales can now be recorded.

1. On the Toolbar, choose the **Gear icon**.

2. Select **Recurring Transactions** from the **Lists menu**.

3. Once you've located your template, choose **Use from the Action selection**.

4. If you want a clearer concept of how your sales receipt ought to appear, feel free to look at the sample breakdown of total daily sales that is provided below.

Recording Bank Deposits

You frequently deposit several payments from different sources at once while making a deposit at the bank. Typically, the bank keeps track of everything as a single record with a single total. The same payments won't match how your bank reported the deposit if you enter them as separate records in QuickBooks.

In these circumstances, QuickBooks offers a unique method for you to combine transactions so that your records correspond to your actual bank deposit. To record bank deposits in QuickBooks Online, follow these steps.

1. To combine transactions, add them to your **Undeposited Funds account**.

2. After that, merge them using the bank deposit tool.

Step 1: Put Transactions into The Undeposited Funds Account

Consolidate any invoice payments and sales receipts you wish, if you haven't already, by placing them into the Undeposited Funds account. This account holds all pending transactions until you're ready to record a deposit. By doing so, QuickBooks manages the process seamlessly, automatically processing and transferring transactions into your designated accounts. While the Undeposited Funds account is optional, it streamlines your workflow and ensures efficient transaction handling.

Step 2: Combine Transactions in Quickbooks With A Bank Deposit

In QuickBooks, each bank deposit creates a distinct record. When making deposits, ensure to follow these steps for each deposit slip:

1. Click on + New.

2. Opt for Bank Deposit.

3. Pick the account for depositing from the Account menu.

4. Tick the relevant box for each transaction to combine.

5. Confirm that the total of selected transactions aligns with the deposit slip amount, using it as a reference.

6. Select either Save and new or Save and close to finalize.

Keeping Tabs on Invoice Status and Receiving Payment

By letting them select the due date when seeing the invoice, Schedule Pay encourages timely payment from your clients. Up until the invoice's due date, your customer may select any day to make a payment.

Set Up Schedule Pay for Your Invoice

The good news is that starting Schedule Pay requires no action on your part. You're ready to go as long as your invoices are configured to accept online payments.

Your clients see the Schedule Pay option when you issue a new invoice after they click the Review and Pay button on their emailed invoice.

Schedule pay won't work if;

- The invoice is Due on receipt.
- Your customer edits the amount to be paid.

- The main amount of the invoice is $50,000 or more.

You can also keep tabs on the scheduled pay status of your customers invoices by taking the steps below;

- Select **Sales**, then **Invoices**.
- Locate the invoice whose payment status you want to verify.
- The activity tracker panel will appear when the status field on that invoice line is selected.

When the Payment Scheduled status appears beneath the section for invoice activity, you know your customer has Schedule Pay set up.

Giving Money Back to a Customer

It occurs. It's unfortunate, but it does happen. There are times when you must refund money that a consumer gave you.

In event that a customer returns goods to you, send a credit memo. As an alternative, you might give a refund receipt if you need to reimburse a customer for their money, possibly because the customer's goods arrived damaged and they don't want to place another order.

Issuing A Refund to A Customer

You can reverse a deposit made by a customer who paid you a down payment on an invoice but later backed out of the deal by offering them a refund and applying for credit.

Create a credit memo, and a check to return the deposit, and then record the payment in QuickBooks Online to refund the deposit.

Step 1: Create A Credit Memo

1. Choose + **New**.

2. Click on **Credit Memo**.

3. Choose the **Customer's name** that appears on your invoice.

4. In the Amount field, enter the invoice's total, including the deposit.

5. Choose **Save**.

Step 2: Generate A Refund Check for The Deposit.

1. Choose + **New**.

2. Choose **Check**.

3. In the **Payee field**, pick the client.

4. Select **Accounts Receivable** from the **Category menu** under **Category Details**.

5. In the Amount area, enter the deposit's total amount.

6. Select **Publish and close**.

Step 3: Record A Payment

1. Choose + **New**.

2. Click on **Receive Payment**.

3. Choose the **Customer's name** that appears on your invoice.

4. Verify that the sum of the credits matches the credit memo and invoice that are mentioned under **Outstanding Transactions**.

5. Check the boxes next to the invoice and credit memo in the Outstanding Transactions section.

6. Select **Publish and close**.

Recording A Credit Memo

Certain clients prefer to receive a credit applicable towards reducing their upcoming invoice balance instead of opting for a refund. QuickBooks offers several methods to manage credits efficiently. One option is to generate a credit memo for an immediate deduction from the customer's outstanding balance. Alternatively, you can input a deferred credit, allowing them to utilize it for future transactions.

Read on for more information on the distinctions and how to use them in client transactions.

You can instruct QuickBooks to automatically apply credit memos to client balances or open invoices if you haven't already. To activate the automatic application of credit memos:

1. Select Account and settings under Settings.

2. Choose the Advanced tab.

3. In the Automation section, click Edit.

4. Select Apply for credits automatically.

5. Pick Save, then click Done.

Recording A Credit Memo

1. Choose + **New**.

2. Click on **Credit memo**.

3. Choose customer's name from the Customer dropdown menu.

4. Enter the credit memo's specifics, including the amount and the date. A custom credit service item can be made, allowing you to rapidly include it as a single line item in credit memos.

5. When finished, choose Save and close.

Chapter 7:

Paying Employees and Contractors

It's a huge choice to decide whether to recruit someone as an employee or an independent contractor. It affects taxes, payroll requirements, and more. There are numerous laws governing this, but here is a brief summary and a list of resources that might be useful.

A person hired by an employer is known as an employee. An employee is typically under more employer control. An independent contractor is a self-employed individual who, typically under their terms, renders services to enterprises.

If your employee is a worker, you must:

- Payroll taxes, such as income, Social Security, and Medicare taxes, should be withheld.
- Pay the same Social Security and Medicare taxes as the employee.
- On employee earnings, pay federal and state unemployment taxes.
- Publish a Form W-2 after the year has ended.

If your employee is a self-employed person:

- Payroll taxes shouldn't be withheld at all.
- Federal and state unemployment taxes shouldn't be paid by you.
- A 1099-MISC form needs to be sent out each year.

Getting Started with QuickBooks Payroll

You have more control and flexibility with QuickBooks Online Payroll's automation and dependability. You'll have more time to devote to giving your clients advice and expanding your business while also letting your clients know that their payroll is handled correctly.

From QuickBooks Online Payroll, you can manage payroll, access health benefits, and provide HR support for your clients.

For smooth business administration, use QuickBooks Time to access accounting, payroll, and time tracking.

Payroll will begin to operate automatically after initial setup. Utilize clear notifications and alerts to stay in control of your finances.

By combining accounting and payroll in one location, you can handle your client's finances with ease.

When you need them, use the integrated suite of QuickBooks products.

Access a full range of employee services, including workers' compensation and health benefits, all administered directly from your payroll account.

You may approve payroll at any moment because of the seamless integration of automated timekeeping provided by QuickBooks Time with QuickBooks Online Payroll.

Eliminate tax penalties, decide how to pay your employees, and set up your own payroll system to position yourself for success.

Payroll taxes are computed, submitted, and remitted automatically at both the federal and state levels.

- Payroll will operate automatically following the initial setup. With simple alerts and messages, Auto Payroll makes it simple to maintain control.
- Pay W2s and 1099 contractors in a single transaction. Online pay stubs are also accessible to employees.

Turning on QuickBooks Payroll

A popup to accept the New Pricing and Billing Terms and Conditions will appear once you log in to your new QuickBooks Online Payroll account. Accept the terms so that your payroll can be processed without interruption. Once the terms and conditions have been accepted, your new billing date will begin.

Below are some icons on the toolbar navigation to help you out;

- **Search**: in this section, you can search for a particular employee or payroll transaction rather than having to make use of the navigation menu.
- Notifications: in this part, you will be able to see all the important reminders or alerts about dates of tax, product news, and more.
- **Settings**: in this part, you can configure your payroll preferences, manage users on your account and also change companies.
- Log in as the **Primary Admin** when **QuickBooks Online** opens.
- Then **click Account and settings under Settings.**
- Choose **Billing & Subscription**.
- Additionally, the name of your salary plan is included in the second box.

The time it takes to enter your payroll information into QuickBooks is something that we are conscious of. A consequence of this is that the setup is designed to enable you to enter information whenever it is suitable for you and to preserve it as you move along.

The tasks can be finished in virtually any order that you put them in. There are a few additional steps that need to be completed if you have already paid your staff for this year.

To do these tasks:

1. Select **Overview** after going to **Payroll**.

2. On assignment you wish to work on, click **Start**.

Setting Payroll Preferences

You can modify the manner in which you keep track of your payroll wages, taxes, deductions, and corporate contributions in your chart of accounts in order to meet the demands of your accounting system.

If you are using Core, Premium, or Elite payroll without accounting turned on, you should check out the **Export your payroll data into QuickBooks feature**. This will allow you to change the accounting settings for your payroll transactions.

Step 1: Determine What Account Type You Would Like to Use for Your Payroll Transactions

Your payroll obligations and expenses are initially tracked in default accounts provided by QuickBooks Online Payroll. Nonetheless, if you prefer, you have the option to establish a new account within your QuickBooks Online Chart of Accounts to separately record them. It's important to note that QuickBooks restricts the use of alternative account types, such as cost of goods sold, for managing liabilities or payroll expenditures.

Step 2: Modify Your Payroll Account Register

If you wish to adjust the account type or name, simply edit the existing entry. Alternatively, if you prefer to allocate a specific payroll item to a different account, you can add a new one.

For guidance on adding or modifying a payroll account, continue reading. Feel free to proceed to step 3 if the desired account is already in your records.

1. Go to the Chart of accounts under Settings.

2. Choose the New option to set up a new one. As an alternative, you can search for the account that you want to modify and then select Edit from the dropdown menu that appears when you view the register. In the event that you see the New category window instead of the Account window, you are in the process of creating a sub-account. Change to accountant view if a new parent account needs to be created.

3. Select Expenses or Other Current Liabilities from the Account Type dropdown menu.

4. Select a Detail type based on the account type you chose.

5. In the Name area, you can add or change the account name.

Step 3: Adjust Your Payroll Accounting Preferences

1. Access Payroll settings via the Settings menu.

2. Choose Edit under the Accounting section.

3. For specific sections, opt for Edit.

4. Pick the appropriate account for the transaction related to the payroll item in question. Then, proceed by clicking Continue.

If you would like to make changes to past transactions;

1. If you would like to make changes to the already existing transactions click on **Edit**.

2. Specify a **Start Date**. With the exception of the Bank Account section, we'll modify every account.

Setting Up Payroll Taxes

The state payroll taxes that you and your employees must pay depend on where your employees live and work. Local taxes, state disability insurance, state unemployment insurance, and paid family leave may all be included in your state taxes.

Following are the steps to add a new state to your payroll product if you have an employee in one.

Step 1: Find Out the State Taxes That Apply and Obtain the Information

Determining the accurate state and municipal taxes can pose a challenge due to the uniqueness of each circumstance and condition. The offices of the state withholding and unemployment insurance, as well as any relevant local tax offices, should be contacted in the areas where your employees live and work. It is recommended that you do this. These organizations can determine which taxes must be paid in accordance with your circumstances and provide assistance in acquiring the account numbers that are required for filing and paying taxes.

You will need to configure the new state in your payroll product, you'll need the following information, depending on the state taxes that apply:

- Account number(s)
- How often you might be required to make tax payments.
- Tax rates.

Roaming Employees

During a given time period, roaming personnel are employed in multiple states. In each state where they work, your employee may be required to pay State Unemployment Insurance (SUI) or local taxes. Only one SUI tax or local tax jurisdiction per employee can be handled by our payroll tools. We advise against applying any workarounds since they can interfere with your state tax forms.

Step 2: Set Up or Make Changes to Your Employees

Once you have determined which state or local taxes you are required to submit and pay, you will be able to either include a new employee or modify revisions to an existing one.

Step 3: Set Up Your New State Taxes

If you would like us to electronically file your paperwork and pay your taxes, you must finish the state tax setup.

You don't need your account numbers to set up state taxes. Until you enter the account numbers, you will have to manually file the paperwork and pay the taxes.

Step 4: Sign New State Authorization Forms

You might be required to sign consent forms before we can file your paperwork and pay your state taxes, depending on your payroll service.

Preparing Payroll

Step 1: Navigate to Payroll

You should head to the "Payroll" tab after signing in to your QuickBooks account to get going.

There is a "Get Started" button if your QuickBooks Online subscription was just purchased. To move on to the following screen, click on it. The system will ask you a few questions when you first sign up for QuickBooks Payroll, such as if you need HR support and whether you need to keep track of employees' working hours.

You can manually choose one of the plan's three payroll alternatives, but these questions will assist match you with the appropriate one. You can sign up for a 30-day free trial of QuickBooks, and it will suggest the best payroll plan for you.

Step 2: Provide Basic Details Regarding Employee Compensation

The system will ask you whether you have already paid staff for the current calendar year in the following stage. You must select "Yes" if you're transferring from a manual system or another payroll program to QuickBooks Payroll.

Keep in mind that later on in the setup process, the system will want you to provide year-to-date (YTD) payroll information as well as tax payments made for each employee. To guarantee that your W-2 forms are accurate at year's end, you must provide information about earlier paychecks that were sent to employees before the start of your QuickBooks Payroll subscription.

You can get detailed pay records from your former payroll provider in addition to getting YTD data from the most recent payroll you submitted for each employee.

The system will ask you to specify the date that you intend to conduct your first payroll in QuickBooks, in addition to payments to employees in the current calendar year. The physical address of the workplace where the majority of your employees are located will also need to be entered.

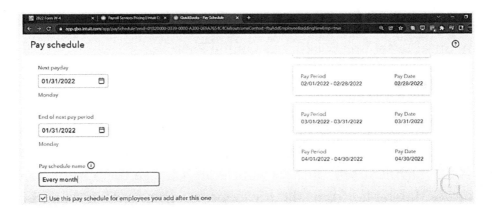

Step 3: Add Employees

When you enter your workplace, a new window that allows you to enter basic personnel data and payroll information into the system will open. To begin entering the necessary information for each person on your payroll, even those who are no longer employed by your business but were paid during the current fiscal year,

- click the Add an employee button.

Step 4: Complete Employee Information

You have the option to enter your employees' email addresses as you enter basic staff information into QuickBooks. This enables the system to send them a link so they may access QuickBooks Workforce, the provider's self-service web portal, to check their pay stubs and W-2s. Even better, the solution has the ability to allow workers to use QuickBooks Time to monitor and record their working hours.

You must complete the employee information fields shown below in order to set up QuickBooks Online Payroll.

Pay Schedule:

- By selecting the **create pay schedule button** under **How often do you pay** (employee), you can specify a payment schedule for your staff. Choose the appropriate timetable from the dropdown menu, which includes options like weekly, twice a month, and monthly. Additionally, you will have the choice of having the plan you just made serve as the standard schedule for subsequent employees who are added to the system.

Employee Pay:

- **How much do you pay** (employee) area, enter the employee's salary. Additionally, you need to provide the staff's default workdays and hours per day.

Employee Deductions/Contributions:

- Select the relevant contributions and deductions in the Does (employee) have any deductions box.

Employee withholding information: Use the data from Form W-4s in the section titled "What are (employee's) withholdings." Choose whether you need the tax form for the current year or one from a previous year when you click "Enter W-4 form." The form changed in December 2020 as of the time of this writing, and QuickBooks keeps both the new and old forms. This makes it possible for you to print one straight from the system to distribute to employees and record the appropriate data.

YTD payroll information: Use the facts from the most recent payroll check to enter the YTD payroll information into the system if you paid the employee this year. The sums paid during the current quarter but before you started using QuickBooks Payroll will also be requested by QuickBooks, so take note of this.

Payment method: There is a dropdown menu in the "How do you wish to pay (employee)" section where you may choose between direct deposit and (manual) check to pay the employee. Utilize the information provided on the direct deposit authorization form along with the voided check obtained from the employee should you opt for direct deposit.

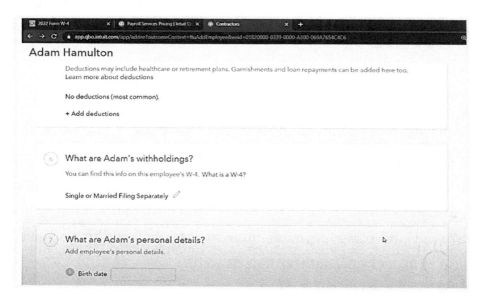

Step 5: Click on "Run Payroll"

- Click the **Run payroll button** in the top right corner of the screen while you are on your "Payroll" dashboard.

Step 6: Insert Current Hours

It should be noted that for salaried employees, the system will automatically fill in the total hours depending on the employee's initial setup's preset amount of work hours. You must manually enter the actual working hours for hourly employees in the "Regular Pay Hrs" column or transfer the time data from your time tracking software to the system.

Your staff's work hours will immediately display in QuickBooks Payroll when you subscribe to the Premium or Elite plans of the software and utilize QuickBooks Time (included in both tiers) to record and track employee attendance. Please feel free to update the system if the staff's working hours change.

Step 7: Review and Submit Payroll

Your final opportunity to evaluate and make changes to the payroll data is at this stage. Check the payment method to make sure that employees who should be paid by direct deposits and paychecks show up correctly, in addition to the number of hours worked and other payment information. Review the employee and employer tax contributions as well.

- Click the **Preview payroll option** at the bottom right of the screen once you have done checking the time data and payment information for your employees.

If everything appears to be in order,

- press the **Submit Payroll button** in the bottom right corner of the screen.

After that, you can print the employees' payroll cheques and/or direct deposit remittance advice. If you use QuickBooks Online as your accounting program, a bill will be generated immediately for each payroll handled, making it simple to reconcile your payroll account.

Recording Payroll Information

Journal entries are a useful workaround for keeping track of the accounting data for your payroll.

An illustration of how to enter a payroll transaction into a journal may be found below.

Example: Five people work for Fred's Residential Remodeling Company. You would use the employees' gross compensation for the journal entry. In this case, the total sum is $4055.00.

1. Click on + **New**.

2. Choose **Journal Entry**.

3. Beneath **Date**, choose **the payroll payment(s) date**.

4. Insert **Entry #** for a journal entry.

5. Debit and Credit accounts:

   - Use a debit expense account to keep track of gross pay. ($4,055.00)
   - Account used to track Employer Contribution is a debit expense (e.g. CPF, EPF, etc.). ($251.41)
   - Payroll deductions are made from a credit bank account. ($4306.41)
   - Note: The next two stages explain how to save the transaction to make entering simpler the next time. Please skip these steps if you just want to complete the transaction once or if you have QuickBooks Online Simple Start.

6. Click on Make Recurring.

7. Insert a memorable Template Name then configure Template Type to Unscheduled; click on Save Template.

8. Choose Save.

Using the same example, the lines on the journal entry would read as follows if the employer was in charge of covering the liability:

1. Use a debit expense account to keep track of gross pay. ($4,055.00)

2. Account used to track Employer Contribution is a debit expense (eg. CPF, EPF, etc.). ($251.41)

3. Medicare spending account used for tracking. ($58.80)

4. Payroll liabilities are tracked using the credit liability account. ($1228.67)

5. By the net amount of the payroll payments, credit the bank account used for processing payroll. ($3136.54)

Currently, $1,228.67 is waiting to be paid in a liabilities account. You would direct the liability account used in the journal entry when writing the checks to settle the responsibility. The responsibility will be eliminated as a result or reduced to the present balance owed.

Enabling Employee Time Tracking

Use this feature to keep track of and charge clients for the time spent on a project or activity. How? Read on.

1. Select Account and settings under Settings.

2. Choose the Time tab.

3. Select Edit in the General or Timesheet section.

4. Decide how you want to log your time;

   o **First day of the work week**: this part affects how employees and contractors see weekly time sheets.
   o **Show service field**: when this is turned on, employees and contractors who complete the timesheets can indicate services that were performed.

- o **Make time billable**: when this is turned on, employees and contractors who complete the timesheets can indicate if activities should be billed to a customer.
- o Show billing rate to users entering time: this section is optional.

5. Click on **Save then Done**.

Once the above settings have been completed, you can now add a time-tracking user;

1. Choose to Manage users under Settings.

2. Choose to Add user.

3. Select Only Time tracking.

4. Choose Next.

5. Locate the worker or vendor you wish to add, click Next, and then fill out their contact information.

6. Choose Save.

Note that A Time Tracking Only user's user type cannot be changed. If different corporate access is required for a time tracker, remove the user and re-add them using the new user type.

Reviewing and Generating Payroll Checks

Regardless of whether you use a different service for payroll alongside QuickBooks for accounting, you are required to continue to keep track of those paychecks in QuickBooks. Third-party paychecks are payments that are produced with sources aside from QuickBooks, like ADP or Paychex. We allude to these payments as "third-party paychecks."

It is possible to import data from paychecks directly into QuickBooks utilizing a number of different payroll systems. If your service provider fails to offer this capacity, we will instruct you on how to manually keep track of these payments as journal entries. Your account information and payroll data are both stored in a single location as a consequence of this.

Step 1: Create Manual Tracking Accounts

Follow the instructions to add additional accounts to your Chart of Accounts if you haven't done so you can keep track of your payroll liabilities and costs.

Make the following expense accounts. Decide on the account type of expense:

- Payroll Expenses: Wages
- Payroll Expenses: Taxes

Step 2: Insert the Payroll Paychecks into Quickbooks Online

Create a journal entry following payment to your staff outside of QuickBooks:

1. Obtain payroll reports or pay stubs for your employees from your payroll service.

2. Navigate to + New.

3. Choose Journal Entry.

4. Input the date of your paycheck in the Journal date field.

5. Optionally, include the paycheck number in the Journal no. area for tracking purposes.

Apply the information from your paycheck report to the entry you are making in your journal. By combining all of the totals of the paychecks that you gave out to employees throughout the pay period into a single journal entry, you can save time and money. There is also the possibility of writing distinct journal entries for every employee if you feel the need to break down the particulars separately.

Establishing or Correcting Payroll Exemptions

Did you know that QuickBooks Online Payroll Core, Premium, and Elite all allow you to adjust previous payrolls? Depending on how the employee was paid and whether any system blocks are in place, you may be able to invalidate, edit, or remove a paycheck.

You can choose to;

- You are required to cancel, edit, and remove any paper paychecks.
- invalid paychecks that were handled by direct deposit.
- You have the option to modify or remove pending direct deposit paychecks.

If you would like to gain access to payroll corrections;

- Locate the Paycheck list page.
- Navigate to the specific paycheck you would like to correct.
- Click on the down arrow on the far right of that row.

The system will automatically recalculate your taxes due after a correction is made and make any required adjustments with the following payroll run.

Printing Payroll Reports

To print payroll reports;

1. The payroll report you want to print is accessible.

2. Select **Share**.

3. Select **the printing options** for your report;

   o **Export to Excel**: Choose this if you wish to print your report as an Excel document. Downloading an excel file, opening it, and printing the report.
   o **Printer Friendly**: Select this option, then choose **Print** to print your report exactly as it appears in your payroll account.

Managing Payroll Taxes

When it's time to pay your payroll taxes, QuickBooks Payroll (QP) informs you of the amount due and assists you in creating the payroll tax papers you need to submit to the appropriate revenue agency.

Paying Payroll Taxes

1. Payroll tax can be found under Taxes so **click on it**.

2. Click on **Pay Taxes**.

3. All unpaid taxes will be shown in this.

4. To record a payment for a tax item, click **Record Payment** to the right of the tax item.

5. After reviewing the data on the following screen, choose **Record and print**.

Viewing Payroll Tax Forms

1. Payroll tax can be found under Taxes.

2. Select Monthly, Annual, or Employer Forms from the Forms area.

3. You can produce quarterly or monthly tax forms and worksheets for monthly forms (i.e. PD7A).

4. You can produce T4s and the T4 Summary report for Annual Forms.

5. You can construct Records of Employment for Employer Forms (ROE).

Paying Contractors

An independent contractor is a self-employed individual who, typically on their own terms, renders services to enterprises.

Setting up 1099-eligible contractors
Add A Contractor as A Vendor

If not already done, add the contractor as a vendor in QuickBooks by following these steps:

1. Navigate to the Payroll section and select Contractors.

2. Click on "Add a contractor."

3. Input the necessary information for the contractor or utilize the "Email this contractor" option to request completion by the contractor.

4. Once done, select "Add contractor."

To monitor payments for 1099 reporting:

Since the contractor has been added as a vendor, it's crucial to track their payments for 1099 purposes. Follow these steps:

1. Access Sales or Get Paid & Pay, then choose Vendors.

2. Locate the profile of the contractor you wish to monitor.

3. Click on "Edit."

4. Ensure to select and check the "Track Payments for 1099" checkbox.

Reporting on 1099 vendor payments
You can use the reports in QuickBooks to assist you to get ready to produce your 1099s. These reports can be run in the following manner to figure out who wants to have a 1099 filed for them.

See All Your 1099 Vendors:

1. Select **Reports** from the Business Overview menu, or click **Report** and look for the Vendor Contact List option.

2. Choose Customize.

3. Select **Change columns** under **Rows/Columns**.

4. Check the box next to Track 1099.

5. Click on **Run Report**.

To see 1099 totals, accounts, amounts, and other details;

1. Select **Reports** from the **Business Overview menu** or go directly to **Reports**.

2. Enter **"1099 Transaction Detail Report**," **"1099 Contractor Balance Detail**," or **"1099 Contractor Balance Summary**" into the search bar.

To see all payments to vendors that have a need to go on a 1099

1. Select **Expenses** under **Transactions**, under **Bookkeeping**, or directly under **Expenses**.

2. Select **Contractors** after choosing **Vendors or Payroll.**

3. When you reach the window titled "Check that the payments add up," click **Prepare 1099** and then select **Continue**.

4. Choose the arrow adjacent to the filter symbol at the top of the table to alter the kind of contractors to 1099 Contractors below the criterion or 1099 Contractors that satisfy the criterion. This will allow you to modify the definition of the contractors.

5. You can now determine which contractors are eligible for 1099.

Preparing 1099s
Utilize the data already stored in your QuickBooks Online accounts to efficiently generate your 1099 forms for IRS compliance. When compensating contractors with cash payments, it's necessary to file 1099 paperwork with the IRS.

Follow these steps to create your 1099s (1099-MISC and 1099-NEC) within QuickBooks Online:

1. Navigate to Contractors or Vendors under Payroll or Get paid & pay.

2. Select Let's get started, then proceed to Prepare 1099s.

3. Ensure that your company's name, address, and tax ID match the details on any tax notices or letters from the IRS.

4. Choose the appropriate boxes corresponding to the types of payments made to contractors throughout the year. Note: Pay attention to recent modifications to 1099 forms. Most businesses typically select "Non-employee compensation (Box 1 1099-NEC)," but consult your accountant if you suspect other payment types.

5. Verify that all contractor information, including email addresses, is accurate.

6. Review payment totals for each selected box from step 4. The system will automatically allocate payments to the appropriate sections of both 1099-NEC and 1099-MISC forms. Proceed to the next step.

Note: Electronic payments made to contractors (e.g., via credit card) may not be visible, as they are often reported by credit card companies or banks. Check the year and threshold above the Name column if any expected payments are missing.

7. Opt to e-file your 1099s by selecting E-File. Alternatively, if you prefer to handle printing and mailing yourself, choose I'll file myself.

Chapter 8:

Reporting and Analysis

It should come as no surprise that you utilize reports to assist you to assess the health of your company. If you keep QuickBooks Online up to date with what you do every day, you are going to be able to make sure that the reports you run have precise details. This is as the reports reflect the information that is contained in QBO.

Types of Reports Available

Profit And Loss Reports: Understanding Income And Expenses
In this section, we will demonstrate how to construct a profit and loss statement to your specifications and how to personalize it. The **profit and loss statement**, which is also known as the income statement, is a financial document that provides information about the profitability of a company during a specific time period. Over the course of a particular time period, this report provides a comprehensive summary of every dollar of revenue and expenditure that have been generated by a particular company. When income is more than expenses, the distinction between the two is reflected on the report as either a net profit (when income is greater than expenses) or a net loss (when expenses are greater than income). As is the case with the

majority of reports, the profit and loss statement can be modified to cater to the requirements of your company.

Here are the steps you need to take in order to produce and personalize a profit and loss statement:

1. From the menu bar on the left, select the Reports option.

2. Choose **Profit and Loss** from the menu that appears once you scroll down to the **Business Overview** section.

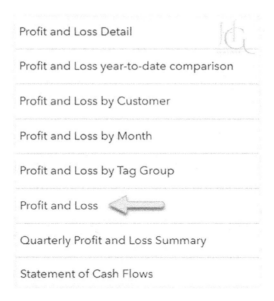

Profit and Loss Detail

Profit and Loss year-to-date comparison

Profit and Loss by Customer

Profit and Loss by Month

Profit and Loss by Tag Group

Profit and Loss ⬅

Quarterly Profit and Loss Summary

Statement of Cash Flows

There are various profit and loss reports available in QuickBooks Online. These include the Profit and Loss Detail report, the Profit and Loss year-to-date comparison, Profit and Loss by customer, Profit and Loss by Month, Profit and Loss by Tag Group, and the Quarterly Profit and Loss Summary, which are preset custom reports.

3. The date range, columns to display, and accounting period can all be specified according to your preferences.

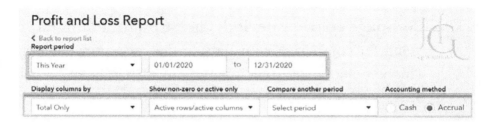

The following is a list of possibilities for simple modification of a profit and loss report, along with a brief overview of each option:

- **Report period**: You have the option of selecting a predetermined time period from the drop-down menu, like this year, and the from and to date fields will be automatically filled in for you. The alternative is to copy and paste the information straight into the from and to date fields.
- **Display columns by**: Whenever it comes to the manner in which columns are displayed, you have a number of different alternatives from which to select. You can choose days, weeks, months, quarters, years, customers, vendors, workers, and products or services from the drop-down menu. You can also specify the date range.
- **Show non-zero or active only**: The purpose of this field is to give you the ability to decide if you would like columns and rows to be shown for all active accounts, irrespective of whether or not those accounts have any activity or include no activity at all. In addition, you have the option of selecting non-zero, which indicates that the report will only include accounts that have a financial value.
- **Compare another period**: Choose from the drop-down menu for comparing your data to that of a previous era. This will allow you to compare your data to some other time.

- **Accounting method**: You have the option of selecting either the cash or accrual accounting method of accounting for which you would like to conduct the report.

The use of number formatting, the selection of rows and columns, the application of filters, and the editorial editing of header and footer information are all further customization options.

An example of a profit and loss report that has been prepared in QuickBooks Online is presented in the following snapshot:

Photos , LLC

PROFIT AND LOSS

January - December 2020

	TOTAL
Income	
Photography Services	22,970.01
Total Income	**$22,970.01**
GROSS PROFIT	$22,970.01
Expenses	
Bank and Credit Card Fees	-27.72
Car & Truck	
Gas	30.15
Total Car & Truck	30.15
Cellphone Expense	550.00
Charitable Contributions	636.00
Continuing Education and Training	100.00
Contractors	500.00
Job Supplies	1,000.00
Meals & Entertainment	228.46
Miscellaneous Expense	487.41
Office Expense	171.00
Office Supplies & Software	477.05
Supplies	389.42
Utilities	320.00
Total Expenses	**$4,861.77**
NET OPERATING INCOME	$18,108.24
NET INCOME	$18,108.24

Photos by Design, LLC had a total income of $22,97001 and expenses totaling $4,86177, which resulted in a net profit of $18,10824 for the period beginning January 1, 2020, and ending December 31, 2020, according to this report on the company's profit and loss. If an income or cost account has a negative balance, it is an excellent idea to click and review every transaction to determine whether or not an item has been classified to the incorrect account. This information may be found by clicking on the account. If you click on a particular number within the report, you will be able to quickly navigate to the specific transactions.

Balance Sheet Reports: Assessing Financial Health At A Glance
At any moment in time, a balance sheet report will provide a summary of the assets, liabilities, and owner's equity that are associated with a particular business. With the help of this report, you will be able to evaluate the **liquidity** of a company, which refers to the availability of cash or assets that can be converted into cash in a short amount of time. This is a significant factor for potential investors and creditors. As is the case with the majority of reports, the balance sheet report can be modified to cater to the requirements of your company. Here, we will walk you through the process of generating the report and customizing it to your specifications.

When you want to create and personalize a report on your balance sheet, follow the instructions below:

1.   Navigate to **Reports** in the left menu bar.

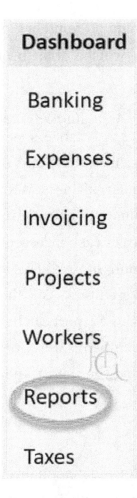

Dashboard

Banking

Expenses

Invoicing

Projects

Workers

Reports

Taxes

2. Scroll down to the business overview section and select
   Balance Sheet.

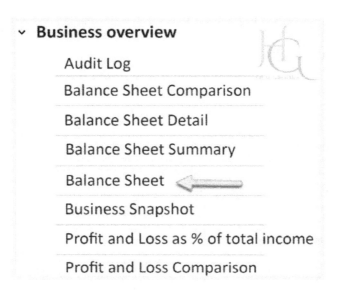

Business overview

Audit Log

Balance Sheet Comparison

Balance Sheet Detail

Balance Sheet Summary

Balance Sheet

Business Snapshot

Profit and Loss as % of total income

Profit and Loss Comparison

There are a variety of various sorts of balance sheet reports that can be generated in QuickBooks Online, as can be seen in the previous sentence. The Balance Sheet Comparison report, the Balance Sheet Detail report, and the Balance Sheet Summary report are all examples of pre-defined custom reports created by the user.

3. You have the ability to personalize the date range, the columns that are displayed, and the accounting period.

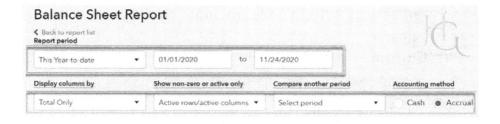

To provide a concise explanation of the fundamental customization choices available for a balance sheet report, the following is a list:

- **Report period**: You have the option of selecting a predetermined time period from the drop-down menu, such as this year, and the from and to date fields will be automatically filled in for you. The alternative is to copy and paste the information straight into the from and to date fields.
- **Display columns by**: Whenever it comes to the manner in which columns are displayed, you have a number of different alternatives from which to select. You can choose days, weeks, months, quarters, years, customers, vendors, workers, and products or services from the drop-down menu. You can also specify the date range.
- **Show non-zero or active only**: The purpose of this field is to give you the ability to decide if you would like columns and rows to be shown for all active accounts, irrespective of whether or not those accounts have any activity or include no activity at all. In addition, you have the option of selecting non-zero, which indicates that the report will only include accounts that have a financial value.
- **Compare another period**: To compare your data to that of a previous era. This will allow you to compare your data to some other time.

- **Accounting method**: You have the option of selecting either the cash or accrual accounting method of accounting for which you would like to conduct the report.

The use of number formatting, the selection of rows and columns, the application of filters, and the editorial editing of header and footer information are all further customization options. An example of a balance sheet report that has been prepared in QuickBooks Online is presented in the subsequent snapshot:

BALANCE SHEET
As of December 31, 2020

	TOTAL
ASSETS	
Current Assets	
Bank Accounts	
Business Checking	15,980.00
Business Savings	8,309.00
WFB Checking	2,464.92
WFB Savings	2,095.00
Total Bank Accounts	**$28,848.92**
Accounts Receivable	
Accounts Receivable (A/R)	4,350.00
Total Accounts Receivable	**$4,350.00**
Other Current Assets	
Inventory Asset	225.00
Total Other Current Assets	**$225.00**
Total Current Assets	**$33,423.92**
Fixed Assets	
Camera	6,000.00
Total Fixed Assets	**$6,000.00**
TOTAL ASSETS	**$39,423.92**
LIABILITIES AND EQUITY	
Liabilities	
Current Liabilities	
Accounts Payable	
Accounts Payable (A/P)	150.00
Total Accounts Payable	**$150.00**
Credit Cards	
Visa Credit Card	1,200.00
Total Credit Cards	**$1,200.00**
Total Current Liabilities	**$1,350.00**
Total Liabilities	**$1,350.00**
Equity	
Opening Balance Equity	22,315.09
Owner's Investment	90.01
Owner's Pay & Personal Expenses	-2,439.42
Retained Earnings	
Net Income	18,108.24
Total Equity	**$38,073.92**
TOTAL LIABILITIES AND EQUITY	**$39,423.92**

The overall assets of **Photos by Design, LLC** are reported to be **$39,42392** in this balance sheet report, while the overall liabilities amount to **$1,35000**. Additionally, the total equity for the period beginning January 1, 2020, and ending December 31, 2020, is **$38,07392**.

After you have gained an understanding of the information that can be found on a balance sheet report and acquired the knowledge necessary to build a personalized balance sheet, the next topic that we will discuss is the statement of cash flows. In this lesson, you will learn how to personalize the statement of cash flows, which provides you with an understanding of the cash flow management of a company.

Cash Flow Statements: Monitoring The Flow Of Cash In And Out
A comprehensive report that illustrates the cash that goes into and goes out of your company over some time is called a statement of cash flows. Operating operations, investment activities, and financing activities are the three divisions that it divides cash flow into. All of the resources that are an aspect of the everyday affairs of the firm are considered to be **operational** activities. These activities comprise things like money owed to vendors (accounts payable) and cash that is owed to consumers (accounts receivable). Among the operations that fall under the category of **investing** is the acquisition of assets for the company, such as a computer. The money that is received from a business loan or line of credit is considered to be part of the **financing** activity.

In a manner analogous to that of the profit and loss and balance sheet reports, the statement of cash flows can be tailored to meet the requirements of your organizational structure. Here, we will walk you through the process of generating the report and customizing it to your specifications.

If you want to develop a statement of cash flows report that is customized to your needs, follow the instructions below:

1. Navigate to **Reports** in the left menu bar.

2. Scroll down to the **Business Overview** section and select **Statement of Cash Flows.**

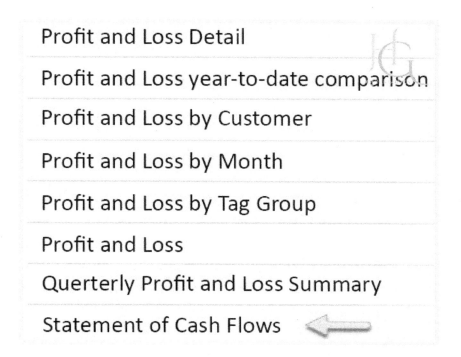

Profit and Loss Detail

Profit and Loss year-to-date comparison

Profit and Loss by Customer

Profit and Loss by Month

Profit and Loss by Tag Group

Profit and Loss

Querterly Profit and Loss Summary

Statement of Cash Flows

3. You can customize the date range and columns to display.

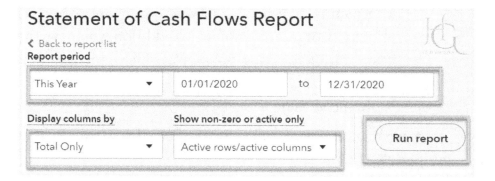

Statement of Cash Flows Report

‹ Back to report list

Report period

| This Year ▼ | 01/01/2020 | to | 12/31/2020 |

Display columns by | **Show non-zero or active only**

| Total Only ▼ | Active rows/active columns ▼ | **Run report** |

A statement of cash flows report can be customized in a number of fundamental ways, and the following are some brief examples of those options:

- **Report period**: You can select a predetermined time period from the drop-down menu (for example, this year), and the from and to date fields will be automatically filled in for you. The alternative is to copy and paste the information straight into the from and to date fields.
- **Display columns by**: When it pertains to how columns are displayed, you have a lot of alternatives from which to pick. You can choose days, weeks, months, quarters, years, customers, vendors, workers, and products or services from the drop-down menu. You can also specify the date range.
- **Show non-zero or active only**: This parameter gives you the ability to choose if you'd like columns and rows to be revealed for each of the active accounts, irrespective of whether or not they have activity or a zero amount. In addition, you have the option of selecting non-zero, which indicates that the report will only include accounts that have a financial value.

4. After making your selections, click the **Run report** button.

5. You will see a statement of cash flows that is comparable to the one that is presented below on your screen:

Photos   LLC

STATEMENT OF CASH FLOWS

January - December 2020

	TOTAL
OPERATING ACTIVITIES	
Net Income	18,108.24
Adjustments to reconcile Net Income to Net Cash provided by operations:	
Accounts Receivable (A/R)	-4,350.00
Inventory Asset	-225.00
Accounts Payable (A/P)	150.00
Visa Credit Card	1,200.00
Total Adjustments to reconcile Net Income to Net Cash provided by operations:	-3,225.00
Net cash provided by operating activities	$14,883.24
INVESTING ACTIVITIES	
Camera	-6,000.00
Net cash provided by investing activities	$ -6,000.00
FINANCING ACTIVITIES	
Opening Balance Equity	22,315.09
Owner's Investment	90.01
Owner's Pay & Personal Expenses	-2,439.42
Net cash provided by financing activities	$19,965.68
NET CASH INCREASE FOR PERIOD	$28,848.92
CASH AT END OF PERIOD	$28,848.92

Photos by Design, LLC has a net cash inflow of **$14,88324** from business operations, a net outflow of cash of **$6,00000** from investments, and a net cash inflow of **$19,96568** from financial operations for the period beginning January 1, 2020 and ending December 31, 2020, according to this Statement of Cash Flows report.

Custom Reports: Tailoring Reports To Specific Business Needs
To obtain the information that you require, you do not have to start from scratch when creating a report in QuickBooks Online; rather, you can modify an existing report to meet your requirements. Any modifications that you do to a report can be

saved, which means that you won't have to start from scratch every time.

If you want to personalize a report, the procedures that you need to take are as follows:

1. To access the report center, head to the left menu bar and click on the **Reports** option. There, you will see the following:

2. Select the report you want to customize. In this case, we will customize the **Profit and Loss** report, as indicated:

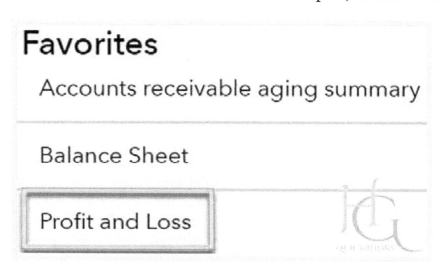

Favorites

Accounts receivable aging summary

Balance Sheet

Profit and Loss

3. Click the **Customize** button located in the upper-right corner:

Customize

4. The following customization window will appear:

Customize report

▶ General

▶ Rows/Columns

▶ Filter

▶ Header/Footer

As indicated in the preceding screenshot, there are four primary areas you can customize:

- General
- Rows/Columns
- Filter
- Header/Footer

Generating and Customizing Reports

In **General** report customizations, you can select the **Report period**, **Accounting method**, and how you would like numbers formatted on any report:

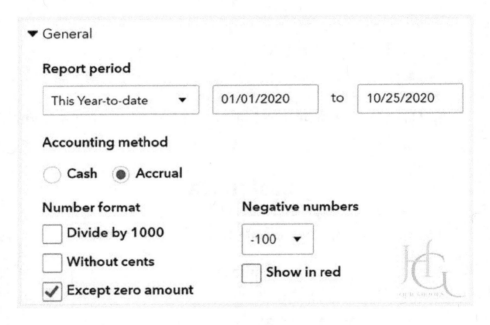

The following is a concise summary of the components that are contained in the general report customization option:

- **Report period**: Choosing the time period that you want to be included in the report is the first step. Either simply putting the dates into the fields or picking the pre-set time frames from the drop-down menu are both viable options for doing this task.

- **Accounting method**: You have the option of selecting the accounting method that you would want to see the report in, which can be either **cash or accrual**. When you set up your QuickBooks account, the accounting method that you selected will be the one that is automatically used for the various reports. You are, however, able to make this modification immediately on the report. Once you have reached the **Company settings** page, pick the **Accounting** tab to make changes to the default accounting method.

- **Number format**: You can format numbers by dividing them by 1,000, deleting the cents, and ensuring that nothing with a zero quantity is displayed.

- **Negative numbers**: You have the option of selecting one of three different ways to display negative numbers and selecting it from the drop-down menu. In addition to being placed in front of the number or behind the number, the negative numbers can also be enclosed in parentheses. For instance, the negative numbers could be written as -100, 100-, or (100).

Given that you are now acquainted with the general report modifications, the next topic we will cover is how to personalize the rows and columns of the report.

Row and Column Report Customization

Rows/Columns: The modification of the report comprises formatting the columns, contrasting the current data to data from a prior period, and comparing the total number of columns and rows to the total number of columns and rows on the report:

A description of what is contained in the Rows/Columns report modifications is provided in the following brief paragraphs:

- **Columns**: This feature shows information about columns by displaying totals only, by period (days, weeks, or months), or by customers, vendors, or workers.
- **Show non-zero or active only**: Choose whether you want to display only non-zero data or all active data (with

and without zeros). In order to maintain the cleanliness and concision of your reports, this choice is advised.

- **Period Comparison**: This feature gives you the ability to see how the current period relates to a previous period, year, or year-to-date of the same period. You have the option of displaying this change in either a percentage format or a dollar figure, or both.

- **% of Row** or **% of Column**: It is possible to view the percentage of every item that appears on the report in comparison to other items that are located on the same row or column of the report.

- **% of Income** or **% of Expense**: If you choose the % of **Income** option, the program will determine the percentage of each item that is shown on the report that contributes to the overall income that is reported. When you select % of **Expense**, you perform a computation that is quite similar to the one described before, except this time you use the entire expenses that have been recorded.

Using Filters to Customize Reports

Additionally, you have the ability to filter reports based on **Distribution Account, Customer, Vendor, Employee,** and **Product/Service** in order to personalize reports for particular data. A tick must be placed in the box to the left of the filter in order to filter a report. After that, you must select the desired filter from the drop-down menu in the following manner:

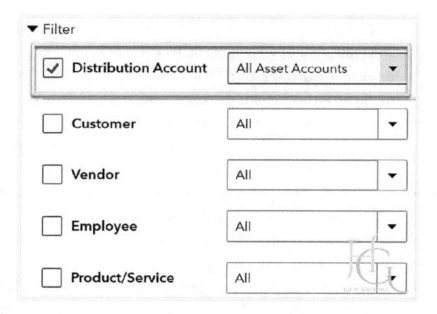

In what follows, a brief description of the components that are contained in filtering reports is provided:

- **Distribution Account**: To choose the account types you are interested in filtering on, click the drop-down arrow and then browse through the available options. Most of the accounts, throughout the balance sheet accounts, most of the asset accounts, and much more are among the alternative choices.
- **Customer**: To pick a particular customer to filter on, click the drop-down arrow. Alternatively, you can choose all of your clients by clicking on the arrow.
- **Vendor**: To select individual suppliers to filter on, click the drop-down arrow. Alternatively, you can select all merchants by clicking the arrow.

- **Employee**: To choose a particular staff member to filter on, or to filter on all employees, click on the arrow that drops down from the window.
- **Product/Service**: To pick individual items and services, numerous products and services, or every item and service, click on the arrow that is located in the drop-down menu.

Header and Footer Report Customization

Additionally, you have the ability to personalize the content that takes up the header and footer of reports. It is possible that this will be helpful in the event that you have filtered a report in a manner in which the present title is no longer relevant.

The header can be customized by adding a logo, updating or changing the name of the company that shows on the report, and changing the title of the report. All of these options are available to you. In addition, you have the option of removing the dates from the report or displaying them on the report.

This is a screenshot of the **Header** information that may be changed on reports, and it is as follows:

Header

☐ Show logo

☑ Company name   Photos By Design, LLC

☑ Report title   Profit and Loss

☑ Report period

In order to personalize the footer, you have the option of deciding whether or not to show the date on which the report was written, the time at which the report was set up, and the rationale for the report.

Take a look at the following example of the Footer information that could be adjusted on reports according to your preferences:

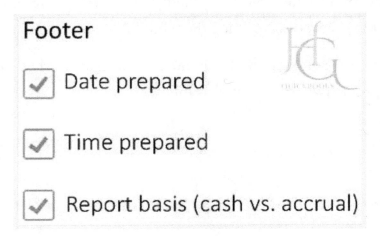

Footer

☑ Date prepared

☑ Time prepared

☑ Report basis (cash vs. accrual)

Saving A Customized Report

After making modifications to a report, you have the option to save those modifications so that they will be preserved the next time you run the report. The **Save customisation** button can be found in the upper-right area of the screen. Make sure to click it whenever you run a report, as demonstrated below:

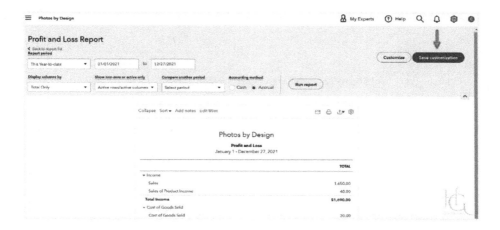

The following is a quick description of every field, in addition to the window that opens for you to select from:

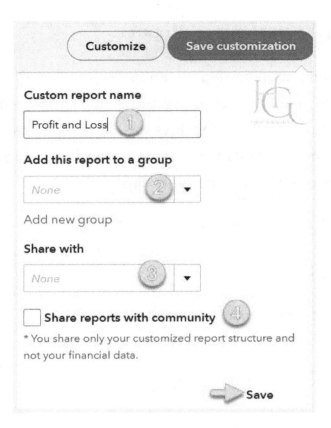

- **Custom report name** (1): This field will display the default report name that was assigned to the report. By including the name of your company to the report, you have the ability to personalize its name. For instance, you could call it **Profit and Loss with Photos by Design.**
- **Add this report to a group** (2): Report groups are utilized in order to execute numerous reports simultaneously. To give you an example, if you regularly run the same five reports when you close the books, you may combine each of the five reports into a group and generate them all simultaneously. To set up a group, click

the **Add new group** button that is located just below the form.

- **Share with** (3): This area gives you the ability to share the report with other users who are affiliated with your organization. You can choose individual people or **All** users by clicking the arrow that drops down.
- **Share reports with community** (4): If you are a member of the QuickBooks community, you have the ability to share the customized reports that you have created with other business owners. The instructions will appear on the screen; all you need to do is click the box that is displayed in the image above.

At this point, you are prepared to learn how to distribute reports because you are aware of how to modify reports so that they meet the requirements of your company. Directly from within QuickBooks, you have the ability to export reports to file formats like as Excel, PDF, or a printer.

When it pertains to exporting the data from your QuickBooks account, you have a number of different alternatives to select from. Any report can be printed out in hard copy, much like the majority of other apps. If you need to make changes to the data or add more information, exporting the data to Excel could be a useful alternative for you to consider. You can save any report as a PDF document and then email it to anyone who doesn't have access to QuickBooks. This is useful in situations where it's necessary to share your data with your accountant, a board member, or anyone else who does not. At long last, QuickBooks comes with the capability to send a report by email.

In the event that you choose the email choice, you will have the ability to send it to several individuals and copy in any additional information that you require. In the event that a report is going to be sent via email, it will be included as a PDF document.

Exporting Reports

When you run a report in QuickBooks, the export data menu will automatically appear in the upper-right corner, as indicated here:

Photos   LLC

PROFIT AND LOSS
January 1 - October 25, 2020

	TOTAL
▾ Income	
Photography Services	22,970.01
Total Income	**$22,970.01**
GROSS PROFIT	**$22,970.01**
▾ Expenses	
Bank and Credit Card Fees	-27.72
▾ Car & Truck	
Gas	30.15
Total Car & Truck	**30.15**
Cellphone Expense	300.00
Charitable Contributions	636.00
Continuing Education and Training	100.00
Contractors	500.00
Job Supplies	1,000.00
Meals & Entertainment	228.46
Miscellaneous Expense	487.41
Office Expense	171.00
Office Supplies & Software	477.05
Supplies	389.42
Utilities	240.00
Total Expenses	**$4,531.77**
NET OPERATING INCOME	**$18,438.24**
NET INCOME	**$18,438.24**

A description of each icon is provided in the following paragraphs:

- **Envelope**: You can send a report right from QuickBooks. This will allow you to send the report by email.
- **Printer**: If you want to print a hard copy of a report, there is a symbol that represents the printer that you can use.

- **Paper**: The icon that is utilized to export reports to Excel or PDF format. It is a representation of a sheet of paper with an arrow passing across it.

Exporting Reports to Excel

The choice of choosing to export reports to Excel is available to you in the event that you require the capability to edit the data on a report or to include extra columns and rows. In order to export a report to Excel, kindly follow the instructions below:

1. Navigate to the reports center by clicking on **Reports** on the left menu bar, as follows:

2. Select the reporting group that includes the report you wish to export, as follows:

3. Choose the report you wish to export, as follows:

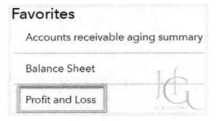

4. The report will appear on your screen:

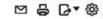

Photos   , LLC

PROFIT AND LOSS
January 1 - October 25, 2020

	TOTAL
▾ Income	
Photography Services	22,970.01
Total Income	**$22,970.01**
GROSS PROFIT	**$22,970.01**
▾ Expenses	
Bank and Credit Card Fees	-27.72
▾ Car & Truck	
Gas	30.15
Total Car & Truck	**30.15**
Cellphone Expense	300.00
Charitable Contributions	636.00
Continuing Education and Training	100.00
Contractors	500.00
Job Supplies	1,000.00
Meals & Entertainment	228.46
Miscellaneous Expense	487.41
Office Expense	171.00
Office Supplies & Software	477.05
Supplies	389.42
Utilities	240.00
Total Expenses	**$4,531.77**
NET OPERATING INCOME	**$18,438.24**
NET INCOME	**$18,438.24**

5. Click on the icon that resembles a sheet of paper with an arrow going through it, as shown below:

6. Choose **Export to Excel**, as follows:

Export to Excel

Export to PDF

7. Your report should appear in Excel, as follows:

Photos _____ , LLC
Profit and Loss
January 1 - October 25, 2020

		Total
ncome		
Photography Services		22,970.01
Total Income	$	22,970.01
Gross Profit	$	22,970.01
Expenses		
Bank and Credit Card Fees		27.72
Car & Truck		
Gas		30.15
Total Car & Truck	$	30.15
Cellphone Expense		300.00
Charitable Contributions		636.00
Continuing Education and Training		100.00
Contractors		500.00
Job Supplies		1,000.00
Meals & Entertainment		228.46
Miscellaneous Expense		487.41
Office Expense		171.00
Office Supplies & Software		477.05
Supplies		389.42
Utilities		240.00
Total Expenses	$	4,531.77
Net Operating Income	$	18,438.24
Net Income	$	18,438.24

At this stage, you can save the report to your computer while making any modifications that are required to it.

In the event that the report does not appear on your computer right away, you ought to look at the very bottom of the screen, where you should see an Excel icon. When you click on it, the report will be displayed in Excel. Any modifications that you make in QBO after exporting a report will not be reflected in the output of the report that was exported.

It is highly recommended that you export the reports to PDF format rather than Excel if you are required to transmit them to individuals who are not affiliated with the company.

Exporting Reports To PDF
You might consider exporting the reports to a PDF file if you need to share them with your accountant, members of your board of directors, or a financial institution. This is an excellent choice. There is no difference between the initial processes involved in exporting reports to Excel and those involved in exporting reports to PDF format.

1. Click on Reports from the menu bar on the left side of the screen. After that, check that you have chosen the appropriate reporting group, and then choose the report that you want to export. Click on the icon that looks like a sheet of paper with an arrow across it once the report has been displayed.

2. Click on **Export to PDF** as indicated here:

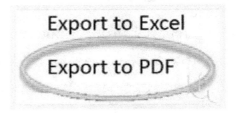

3. The PDF report will appear on your screen, as indicated here:

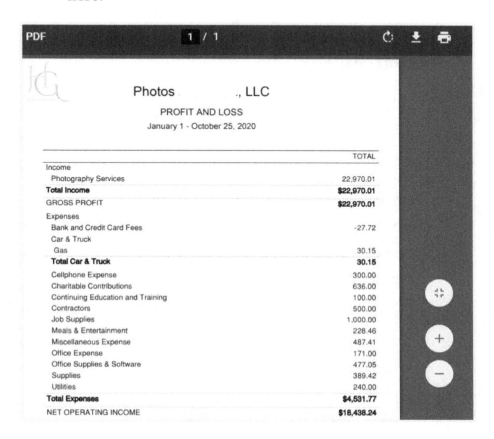

After tapping on the arrow that points down in the upper-right corner of the screen, you have the option of saving the report to your computer. Alternatively, you can print a hard copy of the report by tapping on the print button, as demonstrated in the following example:

Sending Reports Via Email

It is necessary to follow the same procedures in order to export reports to Excel and PDF format in order to send reports via email.

1. Choose the report you want to send by clicking on **Reports** on the left menu bar, ensuring that you have chosen the appropriate reporting group, and then selecting the one you want to send.

2. Once the report has been displayed, select the icon that looks like an envelope according to the following instructions:

3. Click on the **Email** option, as follows:

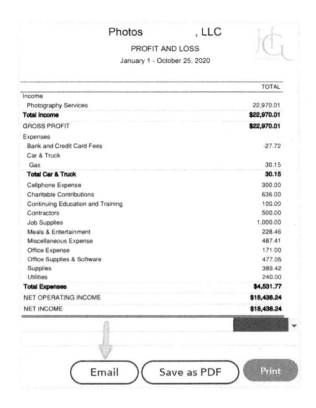

4. The following window will appear:

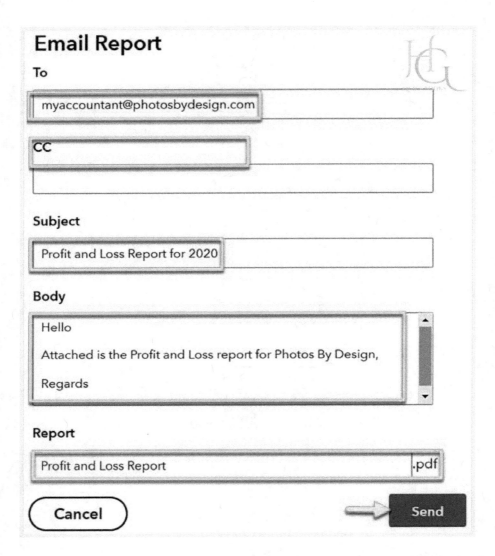

Email Report

To

myaccountant@photosbydesign.com

CC

Subject

Profit and Loss Report for 2020

Body

Hello

Attached is the Profit and Loss report for Photos By Design,

Regards

Report

Profit and Loss Report .pdf

Cancel   Send

A concise explanation of the fields which have to be filled out is provided in the following information:

- **To**: In this area, you will need to enter the email address of each individual recipient. By using a comma (,) following each of the email addresses, you are able to enter several email addresses.

- **CC**: You will need to enter the email address of every recipient who is required to receive a record of the report. Put a comma (,) in between each email address that you want to input in order to enter a number of them.
- **Subject**: The name of the report will be automatically filled in this area when it is submitted.

You can make modifications to this field.

- **Body**: A predetermined message will be automatically filled in this field when you submit your message. You are able to modify the email message so that it meets your requirements.
- **Report**: Please note that the report that you are sending to me via email will be attached as a PDF file.

To send the report via email, click the Send button once you have finished filling out all of the fields.

Analysing Reports for Business Insights Using Excel

A very flexible accounting tool is QuickBooks. Despite all of its features, there are still occasions when we wish MS Excel could be used to perform a few calculations or generate a unique report.

The good news is that you are not forced to pick between them. The program makes exporting reports from QuickBooks to Excel incredibly simple. You may take advantage of all of QuickBooks' benefits while still being able to complete some tasks in Excel.

Automatically Opening Excel Reports Exported from QuickBooks

From a different QuickBooks Online company

1. Log into the account where your lists are stored.

2. Select Reports from Business Overview.

3. Find and run the Account List, Customer Contact List, Supplier Contact List, or Product/Service List reports, depending on the list you need to export.

4. Create a column layout for the list report. Choose each report from the list below to see how the columns should be arranged.

5. Export your report after saving it.

6. Open Excel and the exported report.

7. To remove your company name and the title of the report from the sheet, delete rows 1-4.

8. Your report should now be saved as Excel or CSV.

Sifting Through Excel Reports

Utilize a specified custom field to view each transaction. You could use a custom field you built for a client loyalty program, for instance, to search through all transactions.

Filtering Data

1. Select the magnifying glass-shaped icon for search.

2. Insert the name of the custom field. Select the Gear icon on any page, then choose Custom fields to get a list of your active custom fields.

3. Choose a transaction in the list of results.

4. Select Advanced Search to view the complete list of transactions. From the dropdown menu next to the Contains or Equals field, choose the custom field. Select Search next.

Use custom fields while running reports to gain more insight into your company. For instance, you can filter a report to just display the information that interests you.

Guarding Against Tricky Traps

Two of the largest issues facing small business owners are data security and fraud prevention.

Scammers can use stolen security codes, PINs, and credit card data to conduct fraudulent purchases. A data breach at your small business can result in a variety of different scenarios, including the theft of your Social Security number, your identity, your tax identification number, data mining, and even a lack of control over your accounts.

Small firms are just as vulnerable to a data breach as larger organizations, contrary to popular belief. In fact, when compared to larger enterprises, small businesses lose nearly twice as much money annually, according to the Association of Certified Fraud Examiners.

Slicing Your Data

- Ensure that you are logged in as an administrator to QuickBooks Online.
- You can erase the data for a single QuickBooks Online company using these methods. If you want to completely remove all of your Intuit data, learn more about data management or visit our privacy center.
- Learn more about migrating your lists to a new firm so you can continue using your current lists after starting over.
- Don't use these procedures if you have a QuickBooks Online Accountant. To start afresh, import a brand-new QuickBooks Desktop file.

Creating Custom Reporting with Pivot Tables

1. Access QuickBooks Online by logging in as an administrator.

2. Select Reports from the Business Overview menu, or go directly to Reports.

3. Select Make a fresh report.

4. Type the report's name here.

5. A date range can be chosen from the dropdown.

6. Choose Customize.

7. To expose the available fields, choose **Column**s, search for the subject you wish to report on, and then pick it.

8. Any fields you want to see in the report should be **selected**.

   o It's possible that some fields won't cooperate in a report. Non-compatible fields won't be available when you choose one.
   o Custom fields that you have used show up in this list.
   o To eliminate all fields, choose **Clear All**.

9. Select **Layout**, then select and drag **the listed field**s into the desired order to change the order in which the selected fields display.

10. Utilize a pivot table to add up and total the data in your report.

   o Select the **value field** you wish to summarize after choosing the fields to categorize in the rows and columns.
   o To add a totals row or column, choose **Show totals**.
   o After choosing Rows, Columns, and Values, a pivot table will appear in place of the report view. To restore the report to its default view, toggle off the Show pivot table.

11. To group and subgroup line items by any column, use Group.

- o To compute totals, averages, or percentages for numerical groups, select **Edit group computations**.
- o Select **expand** to see the details inside a group when a report is grouped.

12. To examine only particular entries, use **Filter**. Select **the action**, decide what you want to filter by, and then pick a value from the list. You can use several filters.

13. The Save option will save your report. The report can be changed at any moment.

14. To export the data to a spreadsheet, choose **Export.**

Understanding Pivot Table Requirements

1. The Pivot Table must-have titles for each of its columns.

2. One row should contain only the title.

3. Each item in a column needs to be of the same data type (numbers, dates, or strings).

4. There shouldn't be any merged cells in the data table.

5. Subtotals and grand totals shouldn't be shown in the data table (unless you use a dynamic table).

6. There shouldn't be any empty rows or columns in the table (if an empty row or column remains, Excel will treat the table as 2 different ones).

7. Don't alter the field titles after establishing a pivot table because doing so will cause the values to be lost.

Adding Fields

Once creating a Pivot Table and inputting the fields that you are interested in investigating, you may decide to alter the design and layout of the report in order to create the data simpler to read and scan for specifics. Your ability to change the layout of a PivotTable includes the ability to change the form of the PivotTable as well as the way in which fields, columns, rows, subtotals, empty cells, and lines are displayed. Altering the appearance of the Pivot Table can be accomplished through the utilization of a predefined style, banded rows, and conditional formatting.

1. In the field section, tick the box **next to each field's name**. The field is positioned by default in the layout section; however, you can move the fields around if you'd like.

Through the use of OLAP, date and time hierarchies are automatically included to the Column Labels area. Text fields are included to the Row Labels area, and numeric fields are included to the Values section.

2. After performing a right-click on the field name, choose the necessary command. To position the field in a particular location in the layout section, choose to **Add to Report Filter, Add to Column Label, Add to Row Label, or Add to Values**.

3. When dragging a field between the field section and an area in the layout section, click and hold **the field name** while doing so.

Removing Fields

1. Click on the **Pivot table**. This causes the ribbon's PivotTable Tools tab to appear.

2. If necessary, click **Field List** in the **Show group of the Analyze or Options tab** to show the **PivotTable Field List**. The PivotTable's Show Field List option can also be chosen by performing a right-click.

3. One of the following actions can be taken in the PivotTable Field List to remove a field:

   o Uncheck the box next to the field name in the **PivotTable Field List**.
   o Click the field name in a layout area, then select **Remove Field**.
   o In the layout section, select a field name and hold it while dragging it away from the pivot table field list.

Spreadsheet Sync

1. Go to Data > Pivot table on your Google Sheet after opening it.

2. Choose the data range from which you will build the pivot table. I have chosen the suggested range in this case, which contains all of the sheet's data. Select "OK."

3. To set up the pivot table in the current sheet, select Existing sheet, or to build it on a different sheet, select New sheet. I decided to make the pivot table in the current sheet because this dataset had space for it. Click Create after that.

4. Choose where your pivot table will be placed on the current sheet. Click OK and then Create when you're done.

5. Your pivot table and the Pivot Table Editor should now be visible on the sheet's far right side.

6. You can choose the data to view in the pivot table and how to view it by clicking the Add button that is located next to each table feature. Select the data you want to use in your pivot table by clicking Add next to Row.

7. You can choose how you want to calculate the data in "Values." You can compute and create new values that aren't already contained in your data using the Calculated Field.

Chapter 9:
Acknowledging the Emotional Journey

Embarking on the journey of learning QuickBooks Online can be both exciting and daunting. As you dive into this powerful accounting software, it's essential to acknowledge the emotional journey you may experience along the way. From initial frustration to moments of triumph, every step of the learning process contributes to your growth and mastery of QuickBooks Online.

Addressing Reader Frustrations

Learning any new software can be overwhelming, and QuickBooks Online is no exception. Here are some common frustrations you may encounter and empathetic solutions to overcome them:

- **Complexity**: QuickBooks Online's robust features and functionalities can feel complex at first. Break down learning into manageable chunks, focusing on one feature or task at a time. Utilize tutorials, help articles, and video guides to guide you through the learning process.

- **Confusion with Navigation**: Navigating through QuickBooks Online's interface may initially feel confusing. Take your time to explore the navigation bar, dashboard, and menu options. Practice using keyboard shortcuts and utilize the search function to quickly find what you need.
- **Data Entry Challenges**: Entering data into QuickBooks Online may seem tedious, especially if you're migrating from a different system or dealing with large volumes of transactions. Consider importing data from spreadsheets or bank accounts to expedite the process. Double-check entries for accuracy to avoid errors.
- **Technical Issues**: Technical glitches or connectivity issues can disrupt your learning experience. Stay patient and persistent, and don't hesitate to reach out to QuickBooks Online support for assistance. Keep software and browsers updated to minimize technical disruptions.

Celebrating Small Wins

Amidst the challenges of learning QuickBooks Online, it's crucial to celebrate small victories along the way. Here's why celebrating small wins is essential:

- **Boosts Confidence**: Each small accomplishment, whether successfully reconciling accounts or generating a report, boosts your confidence and motivates you to keep learning.
- **Fosters Progress**: Recognizing progress, no matter how small, keeps you engaged and encourages continued learning and improvement.

162

- **Creates Positive Momentum**: Celebrating small wins creates a positive momentum that propels you forward, even when faced with challenges.

Share your achievements with others, whether it's completing a tutorial, mastering a new feature, or reconciling your accounts for the first time. By acknowledging and celebrating these milestones, you'll build momentum and confidence in your ability to navigate QuickBooks Online effectively.

Establishing a Supportive Community

Learning QuickBooks Online is more enjoyable and rewarding when you have a supportive community to lean on. Here's how to establish and leverage a supportive community:

- **Online Forums and Communities**: Join online forums, social media groups, and community platforms dedicated to QuickBooks Online users. Share your experiences, ask questions, and learn from others' insights and experiences.
- **Local Networking Groups**: Look for local networking groups or meetups for small business owners and entrepreneurs. Connect with peers who use QuickBooks Online and exchange tips and best practices.
- **Training Resources and Workshops**: Attend training workshops, webinars, and seminars offered by QuickBooks Online experts and certified trainers. These

events provide opportunities to learn from experts and connect with fellow learners.

- **Mentorship and Peer Support**: Seek mentorship from experienced QuickBooks Online users or find a study buddy to learn alongside. Peer support can provide valuable encouragement, accountability, and guidance throughout your learning journey.

By establishing connections within a supportive community, you'll gain valuable insights, receive encouragement during challenging times, and celebrate successes together. Remember, you're not alone on your QuickBooks Online journey—lean on your community for support and inspiration.

Chapter 10:

Setting Expectations

Embarking on the journey of mastering QuickBooks Online is an exciting endeavor that holds immense potential for improving your business's financial management. However, it's essential to set clear expectations, nurture a gradual learning approach, and address common concerns to ensure a successful and rewarding learning experience.

Clarifying Reader Commitment

Mastering QuickBooks Online requires a significant level of commitment and dedication. Here's what readers can expect in terms of time investment and commitment:

- **Time Investment**: Learning QuickBooks Online is a process that takes time. Readers should be prepared to dedicate consistent time each week to learning and practicing new concepts and features. While the exact time investment may vary depending on individual learning styles and prior experience, a regular commitment to learning is essential for mastery.
- **Dedication to Practice**: Beyond initial learning sessions, readers must commit to practicing regularly within the QuickBooks Online platform. Hands-on

practice is crucial for reinforcing learning, building confidence, and mastering the software's functionalities.

By setting clear expectations regarding time investment and dedication, readers can approach their QuickBooks Online learning journey with realistic goals and a mindset geared towards success.

Nurturing a Gradual Learning Approach

A gradual learning approach is key to developing a deep and sustained understanding of QuickBooks Online. Here's why it's beneficial and how readers can embrace this approach:

- **Sustained Understanding**: Rushed learning often leads to superficial understanding and retention of information. By taking a gradual approach, readers can delve deeper into concepts, reinforce learning through practice, and develop a solid foundation of understanding.
- **Steady Progress**: Learning QuickBooks Online is a journey, not a race. Encourage readers to focus on steady progress rather than trying to learn everything at once. Break down learning into manageable chunks, prioritize key concepts, and celebrate small victories along the way.
- **Long-Term Success**: A gradual learning approach sets the stage for long-term success with QuickBooks Online. By building a strong foundation of knowledge and skills gradually, readers can adapt to new challenges, master advanced features, and continue to grow and evolve as proficient users.

Encourage readers to embrace patience, persistence, and a willingness to learn gradually, knowing that sustained effort and progress will lead to mastery over time.

Addressing Common Concerns

It's natural for readers to have concerns about the complexity of QuickBooks Online. Here are some common concerns and practical tips for overcoming them:

- **Overwhelm with Features**: QuickBooks Online offers a wide range of features, which can feel overwhelming at first. Encourage readers to start with the basics and gradually explore additional features as they become more comfortable with the platform.
- **Fear of Making Mistakes**: Fear of making mistakes is common when learning new software. Assure readers that making mistakes is part of the learning process and encourage them to embrace a growth mindset. Remind them that mistakes provide valuable learning opportunities and are essential for growth and improvement.
- **Time Constraints**: Many readers may worry about finding the time to learn QuickBooks Online amidst their busy schedules. Encourage readers to prioritize learning by scheduling dedicated time for learning sessions and practice. Consistency is key, even if it means starting with just a few minutes each day.

By addressing common concerns and providing practical tips for overcoming them, readers can approach their QuickBooks Online learning journey with confidence and resilience.

Conclusion

Manage your business seamlessly with QuickBooks Online, a comprehensive small business accounting solution available as an app. Trusted by over 4.5 million users, QuickBooks offers intuitive tools to streamline your company operations. From financial management to invoicing, inventory tracking, and payroll processing, QuickBooks Online has you covered. Integrated payment services ensure efficiency, saving you time and facilitating swift payments. Plus, you can experience its benefits risk-free with a 30-day trial.

QuickBooks simplifies daily tasks with its user-friendly interface. It includes project management features to handle contracts and projects, allowing you to track profits and losses effectively. Organize your business documents such as delivery notes and purchase orders effortlessly. Generate sales orders and acknowledge new customer orders with ease.

As an accounting software, QuickBooks aids in organizing various aspects essential for large companies, including chart of accounts creation, product pricing entries, inventory management, and cost tracking for sales and purchases. It also assists in calculating employee man-hour costs for specific contracts or projects, ensuring efficient project completion.

If you haven't already, sign up for QuickBooks Online today and discover its remarkable benefits for your business!